The Encyclopedia of Collectibles

TIME
LIFE
BOOKS ®

Other Publications:
Library of Health
Classics of the Old West
The Epic of Flight
The Good Cook
The Seafarers
The Great Cities
World War II
Home Repair and Improvement
The World's Wild Places
The Time-Life Library of Boating
Human Behavior
The Art of Sewing
The Old West
The Emergence of Man
The American Wilderness
The Time-Life Encyclopedia of Gardening
Life Library of Photography
This Fabulous Century
Foods of the World
Time-Life Library of America
Time-Life Library of Art
Great Ages of Man
Life Science Library
The Life History of the United States
Time Reading Program
Life Nature Library
Life World Library
Family Library:
   How Things Work in Your Home
   The Time-Life Book of the Family Car
   The Time-Life Family Legal Guide
   The Time-Life Book of Family Finance

The Encyclopedia of Collectibles

Cookbooks to Detective Fiction

TIME-LIFE BOOKS, ALEXANDRIA, VIRGINIA

Time-Life Books Inc.
is a wholly owned subsidiary of
TIME INCORPORATED

Founder: Henry R. Luce 1898-1967

Editor-in-Chief: Henry Anatole Grunwald
President: J. Richard Munro
Chairman of the Board: Ralph P. Davidson
Executive Vice President: Clifford J. Grum
Chairman, Executive Committee: James R. Shepley
Editorial Director: Ralph Graves
Group Vice President, Books: Joan D. Manley
Vice Chairman: Arthur Temple

TIME-LIFE BOOKS INC.
Managing Editor: Jerry Korn
Executive Editor: David Maness
Assistant Managing Editors: Dale M. Brown (planning), George Constable, Thomas H. Flaherty Jr. (acting), Martin Mann, John Paul Porter
Art Director: Tom Suzuki
Chief of Research: David L. Harrison
Director of Photography: Robert G. Mason
Assistant Art Director: Arnold C. Holeywell
Assistant Chief of Research: Carolyn L. Sackett
Assistant Director of Photography: Dolores A. Littles

Chairman: John D. McSweeney
President: Carl G. Jaeger
Executive Vice Presidents: John Steven Maxwell, David J. Walsh
Vice Presidents: George Artandi (comptroller); Stephen L. Bair (legal counsel); Peter G. Barnes; Nicholas Benton (public relations); John L. Canova; Beatrice T. Dobie (personnel); Carol Flaumenhaft (consumer affairs); James L. Mercer (Europe/South Pacific); Herbert Sorkin (production); Paul R. Stewart (marketing)

The Encyclopedia of Collectibles
Chief Researcher: Phyllis K. Wise
Researchers: Charlotte A. Quinn, Trudy Pearson, Judith W. Shanks
Editorial Assistant: Susan Sivard

Editorial Production
Production Editor: Douglas B. Graham
Operations Manager: Gennaro C. Esposito, Gordon E. Buck (assistant)
Assistant Production Editor: Feliciano Madrid
Quality Control: Robert L. Young (director), James J. Cox (assistant), Daniel J. McSweeney, Michael G. Wight (associates)
Art Coordinator: Anne B. Landry
Copy Staff: Susan B. Galloway (chief), Peter Kaufman, Cynthia Kleinfeld, Celia Beattie
Traffic: Kimberly K. Lewis
Correspondents: Elisabeth Kraemer (Bonn); Margot Hapgood, Dorothy Bacon, Lesley Coleman (London); Susan Jonas, Lucy T. Voulgaris (New York); Maria Vincenza Aloisi, Josephine du Brusle (Paris); Ann Natanson (Rome). Valuable assistance was also provided by: Judy Aspinall, Karin B. Pearce (London); Carolyn T. Chubet, Miriam Hsia, Christina Lieberman (New York); Mimi Murphy (Rome).

The Encyclopedia of Collectibles
was created under the supervision
of Time-Life Books by
TREE COMMUNICATIONS, INC.
President: Rodney Friedman
Publisher: Bruce Michel
Vice President: Ronald Gross
Secretary: Paul Levin

The Encyclopedia of Collectibles
Editor: Andrea DiNoto
Art Director: Sara Burris
Assistant Text Editor: Linda Campbell Franklin
Photographers: David Arky, Steven Mays
Assistant Editor: Cathy Cashion
Assistant Art Director: Christopher Jones
Chief Researcher: Catherine Ireys
Researchers: Anna-Teresa Callen, Alix Gudefin, Laura James, Enid Klass, Judson Mead, Barbara Moynehan, Dennis Southers, Henry Wiencek
Administrative Assistants: Eva Gold, Silvia Kelley
Writers: Hyla M. Clark, Hilary Ostlere, Jerry E. Patterson, Alexander G. Sidar III, Susan Teller, Bibi Wein

Editorial Consultant: Jay Gold
Consultants for this volume: George Lang, Louis Szathmáry (Cookbooks); Homer Babbidge (Corkscrews); Norman Cohen, Bob Pinson (Country Music); Katherine R. Koob, Helene Von Rosenstiel (Coverlets); Joe Gish (Cowboy Gear); Rosemary Sullivan (Crèches); Albert Baragwanath (Currier & Ives); Freda Lipkowitz (Cut Glass); George Starr Jr. (Decoys); Ray Goggin, Toni Hechtman, Nora Koch, Warren Thomas, Hazel Marie Weatherman (Depression Glass); Carol Brener (Detective Fiction)

The Cover: Costumes, sheet music, pictures, ball dance cards, books and especially programs and advertising fliers are among the varied items sought by dance-memorabilia collectors *(page 114).*

Acknowledgments: Lyrics from "T.B. Blues" by Jimmie Rodgers and R. Hall, page 29, copyright 1931 by Peer International Corporation, copyright renewed, used by permission; Bob Wills record and Bill Monroe photo, page 42, and Delmore Brothers photo and Hank Williams songbook, page 43, courtesy of Bluegrass Club of New York; Hank Williams record, page 43, courtesy of Country Music Foundation Library and Media Center, Nashville, Tennessee; Jacquard loom, page 49, courtesy of Culver Pictures, Inc.; crèche, page 77, bottom, courtesy of Georges Gudefin; Currier & Ives print, pages 92-93, courtesy of Kennedy Galleries, New York; all other Currier & Ives prints, courtesy of Electronic Race Patrol, Inc.; cut-glass goblet and platter, pages 108-109, courtesy of The Corning Museum of Glass; cut-glass decanter, page 109, courtesy of Phelps Warren; Miró poster, page 116, bronze figurine, page 118, photo of Doris Humphrey, page 124, and photo, page 125, courtesy of The Ballet Shop, New York; set and costume designs, pages 122-123, courtesy of Paul Stiga; photo of Ruth St. Denis, page 124, courtesy of Anne B. Landry; ancient American Indian decoy, page 130, courtesy of Museum of The American Indian, Heye Foundation; fish decoys, page 134, courtesy of Charles F. Hart.

For information about any Time-Life book, please write:
Reader Information
Time-Life Books
541 North Fairbanks Court
Chicago, Illinois 60611

Library of Congress Cataloguing in Publication Data
(The encyclopedia of collectibles)
Includes bibliographies.
1. Americana. 2. Antiques—United States.
I. Time-Life Books.
NK805.E63   745.1'09 0973   77-99201
ISBN 0-8094-2764-8
ISBN 0-8094-2763-X lib. bdg.
ISBN 0-8094-2762-1 retail ed.

© 1978 Time-Life Books Inc. All rights reserved. No part of this book may be reproduced in any form or by any electronic or mechanical means, including information storage and retrieval devices or systems, without prior written permission from the publisher, except that brief passages may be quoted for reviews.
Third printing. Revised 1981.
Published simultaneously in Canada.
School and library distribution by Silver Burdett Company, Morristown, New Jersey.

TIME-LIFE is a trademark of Time Incorporated U.S.A.

Printed in U.S.A.

Contents

- 6 Cookbooks
- 20 Corkscrews
- 28 Country Music
- 44 Coverlets
- 60 Cowboy Gear
- 72 Crèches
- 82 Currier & Ives
- 100 Cut Glass
- 114 Dance Memorabilia
- 128 Decoys
- 140 Depression Glass
- 152 Detective Fiction

Cookbooks
The Choice of the Choice Recipes

Cookbook collectors share with all collectors the excitement of finding a rarity and with all book collectors the joy of discovering a scarce first edition in splendid shape. But they also find it exciting to learn from a book something new about the history of preparing food, or the culinary philosophy of a fine but unfamiliar cook, or a recipe so enticing it propels them to the stove at once. Most cookbook collectors are dedicated cooks. So they buy important new books as well as search out significant old ones.

To be sure, we do not suggest taking a first edition of Amelia Simmons' *American Cookery* into the kitchen to

---

Reading, traveling and cooking are the favorite pastimes of Walter Fillin, a retired executive, and his wife Lucille, a former nutritionist. Both have studied cooking in Paris.

---

risk a butter stain—Simmons' first edition, published in 1796, sold at auction in 1977 for $3,000. If we want to cook from a Simmons recipe we use our copy of a modern reprint. Such reissues, some of them photographic facsimiles of the originals, become important parts of cookbook collections. Many facsimiles were published in fairly limited numbers and are collectible now because of their relative scarcity as well as historical interest.

The earliest cookbook of the Western world was assembled in manuscript form, largely from recipes attributed to a First Century Roman gourmet, Apicius. A modern edition, *The Roman Cookery Book*, published in London in 1958, has parts in Latin accompanied by translations. Among old American cookbooks reproduced in facsimile are *The Virginia Housewife, or Methodical Book of 1824* by Mary Randolph, reissued in 1972, and a 1788 book with a mouth-filling title—the Reverend Dr. John Trusler's *The Honours of the Table or Rules for Behaviour During Meals; with the Whole Art of Carving, Illustrated by a Variety of Cuts*—reissued in facsimile in 1932 with a more modest title, *The Art of Carving*.

Prices of first editions of these early American cookbooks run high—they have fetched thousands of dollars at auctions. Even later editions command $50 and more. But beginning with books published in the late 1800s, famous works—many still in use—can be found. The first editions are the most sought after, of course, and the "firsts" of the two acknowledged classics of American cookbooks have brought high figures at auction: these are the Fannie Farmer *Boston Cooking-School Cook Book* (1896) and Irma Rombauer's *Joy of Cooking* (1931). Much easier to find are the later editions.

Collectors make sharp distinctions between the many editions and countless printings that have put more than three million copies of Fannie Farmer, for example, into circulation. Most prized after the first edition, which shows a copyright date of 1896, are the editions that appeared while the author was still presiding over the reprinting. A total of 10 editions were printed between 1896 and 1914, when Fannie Farmer died. All of these are considered more collectible than the editions that appeared between 1915 and 1929 under the supervision of Cora Perkins, Fannie Farmer's sister. In turn, the Cora Perkins books are considered more collectible than those prepared by Fannie Farmer's nephew, Dexter Perkins, who was in charge for a little over 20 years, between 1930 and 1951. Cora's books show her name as copyright owner; when Dexter took over, his name was used. After 1951, a new name appeared on the title page, which thereafter noted that the book was "Revised by Wilma Lord Perkins," Dexter's wife. These are least valuable on the scale of collectible Fannie Farmers.

The publishing history of *The Joy of Cooking* is shorter. The rare first edition is easy to spot: it was copyrighted in 1931 and was privately printed by the A. C. Clayton Printing Co. of St. Louis, whose name appears on the copyright page. The 1936 edition was the first to carry the name of a commercial publisher, The Bobbs-Merrill Company, Inc. Editions published in 1951 and afterward, recognizable by their copyright dates, are considered less collectible because they were produced under the direction of Mrs. Rombauer's daughter.

The first editions of books by some contemporary writers are valued as collectibles even while later editions of the works are still being sold in stores. Among the most notable of these writers are Julia Child, M. F. K.

The 19th Century French painter Henri de Toulouse-Lautrec was a gourmet and an excellent chef. His friend Maurice Joyant compiled and published the artist's favorite recipes in 1930. The 1966 American edition pictured has illustrations based on Lautrec lithographs.

Toulouse-Lautrec   Maurice Joyant
The Art of Cuisine

Fisher, George Lang, James Beard and Simone Beck. Often a first edition of a cookbook is so small that it sells out almost at once. This was true of George Lang's *Cuisine of Hungary (page 11),* for example. The edition first published by Atheneum in 1973 is no longer available; a cheaper edition published by Crown Publishers is.

Lang's book concentrates on one kind of cooking, and such specialized works are often the easiest and most interesting to collect. Books have been written on every conceivable—and even inconceivable (*The I Hate To Cook Book* by Peg Bracken)—aspect of cooking, and it is simple to decide on an area in which to begin a collection.

One interesting American specialty is charity cookbooks, published to raise money for good causes. They tend to be scarce, for old ones were seldom kept—even by local libraries. Many provide personal and regional recipes not found elsewhere: huckleberry pudding and woodchuck stew, for example. Many cooks revealed the secrets of their most cherished recipes for the first time in aid of charity.

The most successful charity cookbook of all time is probably *The Settlement Cookbook, or The Way to a Man's Heart,* compiled by Mrs. Simon Kander and first published in 1901. Originally, the proceeds went to the Milwaukee Settlement House for Immigrants—hence the title—but later the money was divided among Milwaukee charities serving many different purposes. Collectors look for two *Settlement* editions: the first, copyrighted in 1901, and the one known as the Liberty Edition, put out during World War I, in 1915. The Liberty Edition had a supplement on food conservation, with recipes from government bulletins.

Valuable copies of specialized and general cookbooks can be uncovered almost anywhere, since people generally push old cookbooks into cupboard corners. But one rich source is the book fairs sponsored by college alumni groups, churches and libraries—all of which seem to have many bookish members interested in cooking.

When you turn up an old cookbook, examine it carefully for bonuses. We have found herbs pressed between the pages of some, and often valuable emendations to the recipes: "My grandmother left out the molasses and put in honey." "Add some more cocoa."

Our favorite marginal note is one that asks a question raised by many 19th Century books. For some reason books published in the 1800s have many recipes associated with the name Edith: Edith's cookies, Edith's rhubarb pie, etc. A former owner of one of our books asked in a marginal note: "Who is Edith?"

For related material see the articles on Books and Kitchen Equipment in separate volumes of this encyclopedia.

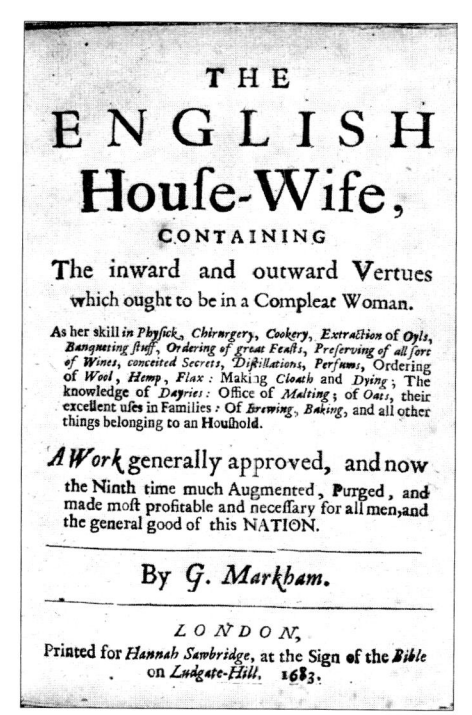

The 1683 ninth edition of the rare "The English House-Wife" by Gervase Markham was little changed from the original (1615), despite the "Augmented" and "Purged" claims.

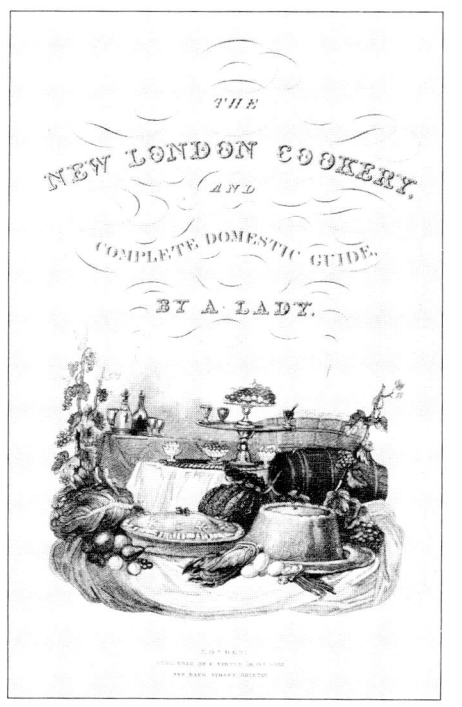

An anonymous English cookbook of about 1827, like most general cookbooks, gives advice on kitchen equipment, hints on health and menus for a whole year in addition to recipes.

"The English Bread-Book" by Eliza Acton appeared in 1857. An aspiring poet, the author was unable to get anything published but her cookbooks; this one was a bestseller.

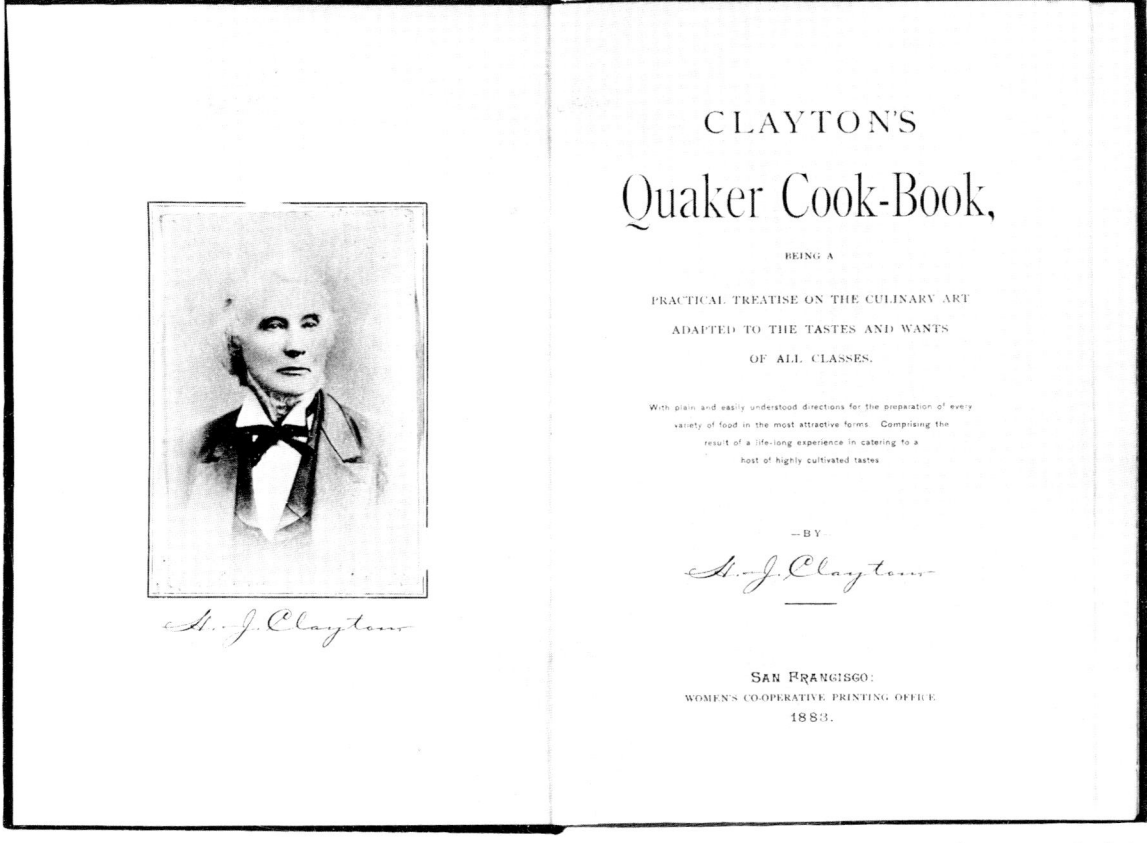

One of the first women's publishing cooperatives published "Clayton's Quaker Cook-Book" in 1883. The frontispiece portrait is of author H. J. Clayton, who wore men's clothes, she said, to gain respect in the San Francisco business world.

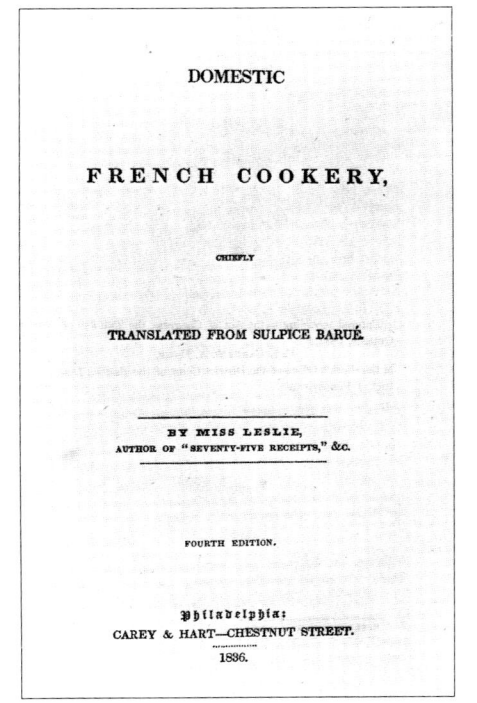

Eliza Leslie was the best-selling author of early-19th Century cookbooks in the United States. She was the first American to offer her countrywomen the wonders of Gallic cuisine.

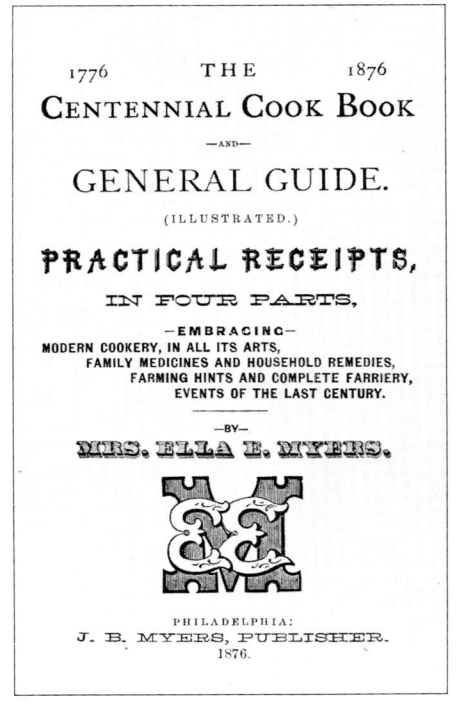

Ella Myers, like many other authors of "practical receipt" books, included family medication advice plus guidance for farmers in her Centennial volume, now rare.

Best known for her "Boston Cooking-School Cook Book," Fannie Farmer tried to improve tasteless recipes ". . . for the Sick and Convalescent" in a book published when she was ill.

10 / COOKBOOKS

A turbot looked like this, adorned with mushrooms on skewers, on the table of Baroness Rothschild in the early 19th Century. The illustration comes from "L'Art de la Cuisine Française au XIXe Siècle," published in 1833 by Antonin Carême, chef to many notables.

Many admirers of classic French cuisine consider Edouard Nignon the premier authority of the 20th Century, and his book, published in 1926, is also prized for its handsome typography.

Collectors value not only books but menus prepared for dinners of historical note. This menu was for a dinner honoring Charles Dickens during his 1867-68 American tour, at Delmonico's in New York.

COOKBOOKS / 11

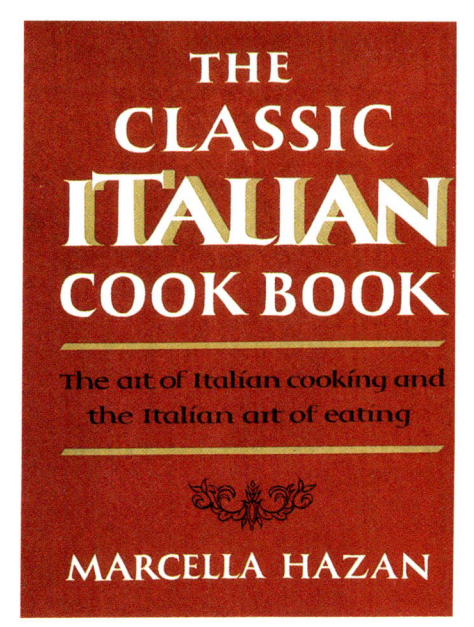

Of the national and regional cookbooks, Marcella Hazan's, focusing on Northern Italian recipes and published in 1973, is one of the best known, making it a prize collectible.

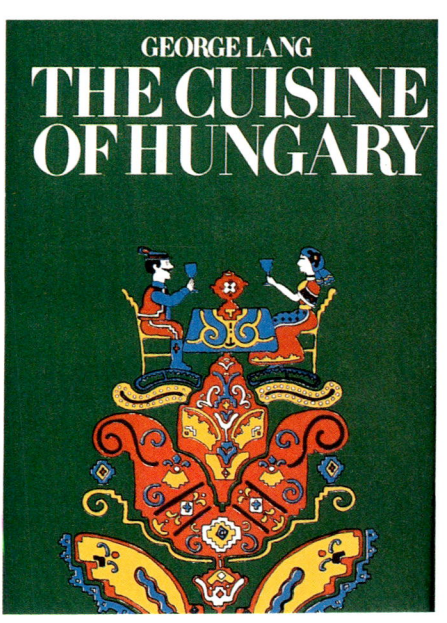

Relatively few first-edition copies were printed of George Lang's 1971 guide to Hungarian cooking. The recipes range from the simple fare of shepherds long ago to modern dishes.

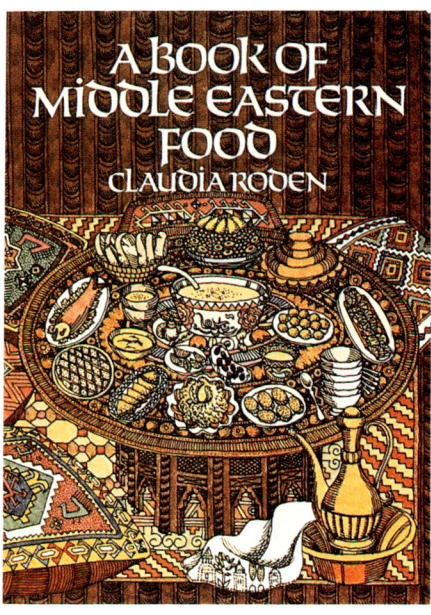

"A Book of Middle Eastern Food," published in Britain in 1968 and in an American edition four years later, is a comprehensive survey of the region's recipes and culture.

Beef with Oyster Sauce

1 lb. beef
2 T. soy sauce
1 T. wine
1 t. cornstarch
5 T. oil
2 T. canned oyster sauce
1 t. sugar
16 canned chestnuts

Cut beef into bite-size pieces and marinate in soy sauce, wine and cornstarch for 5 minutes. Heat oil and sauté over high heat until color changes. Add oyster sauce and sugar and mix well. Serve hot, garnished with chestnuts. SERVES 4

The moon is thought to be most beautiful on the fifteenth day of the eighth month according to the old Chinese calendar. Moon-viewing parties are held where people enjoy chrysanthemums, poetry and moon cakes. During the Yuan dynasty when the Mongols controlled China, armed guards were placed among the people and one cooking knife was tied to a well in a central location to be shared by ten families. The Mongols hoped to protect themselves against rebellions in this way. The Chinese knew that they must attack suddenly and simultaneously if they were to overwhelm the armed guards. Small pieces of cloth on which the date of the planned attack had been written were placed in moon cakes and distributed widely. The successful attack was on August 15. *From top to bottom:* Chilled Pork Kidney with Carrot (Page 81), Squid with Green Peppers and Mushrooms (Page 75), Steamed Crab (Page 74), and Moon Cakes (Page 122).

76

"Mrs. Ma's Favorite Recipes" are Chinese, but their author once taught cooking to the young ladies of the Japanese imperial household.

12 / COOKBOOKS

Many of the cookbooks published to raise money for worthwhile causes, like this one for the Jackson, Mississippi, Symphony League, contain material by writers famous for other literary works. This book, for example, has an introduction by novelist Eudora Welty.

A cookbook issued in 1917 by the Thrift Committee of the National League for Women's Service in Bronxville, New York, suggested substitutions to aid in wartime food conservation, such as bran for flour and lard for butter.

The Cesar of the title shown at right is Cesar Chavez, leader of the West Coast farm workers' union—a pun on the famous salad named for the Caesar Hotel in Tijuana, Mexico.

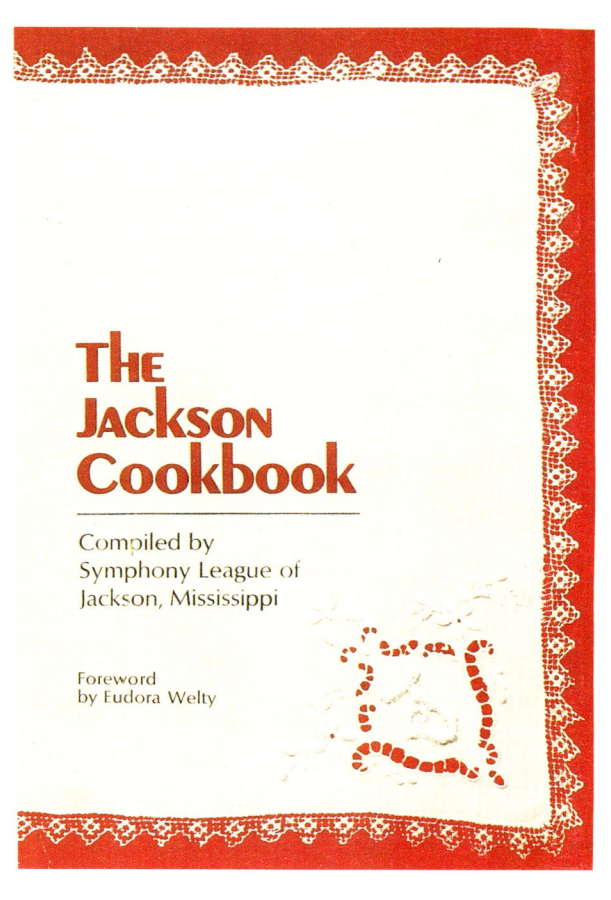

COOKBOOKS / 13

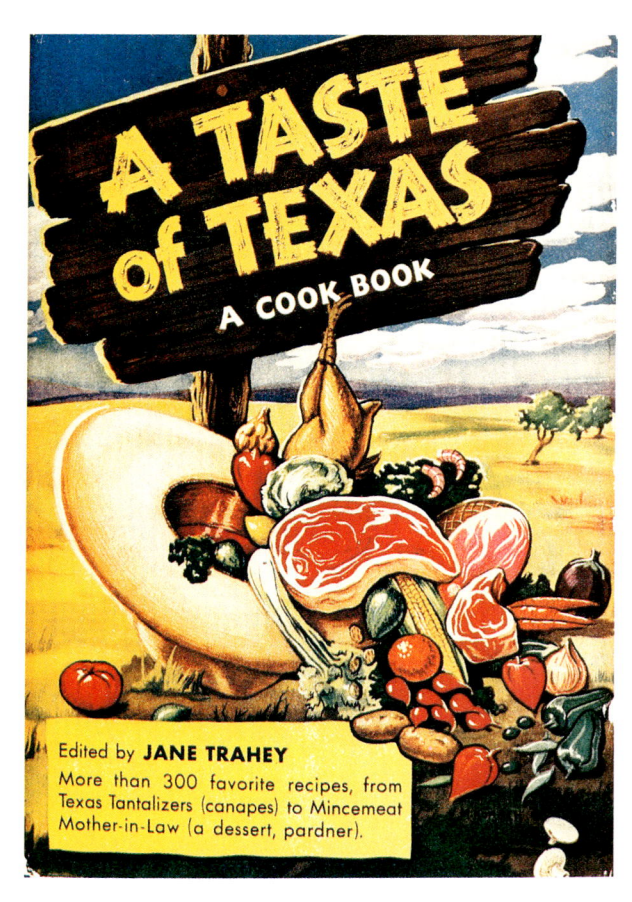

Unique recipes and local folksy touches distinguish regional cookbooks such as the one at left, which includes jerked deermeat and Hopkins County stew, a dish for 50 people that mixes quail, squirrel, chicken, pork and beef.

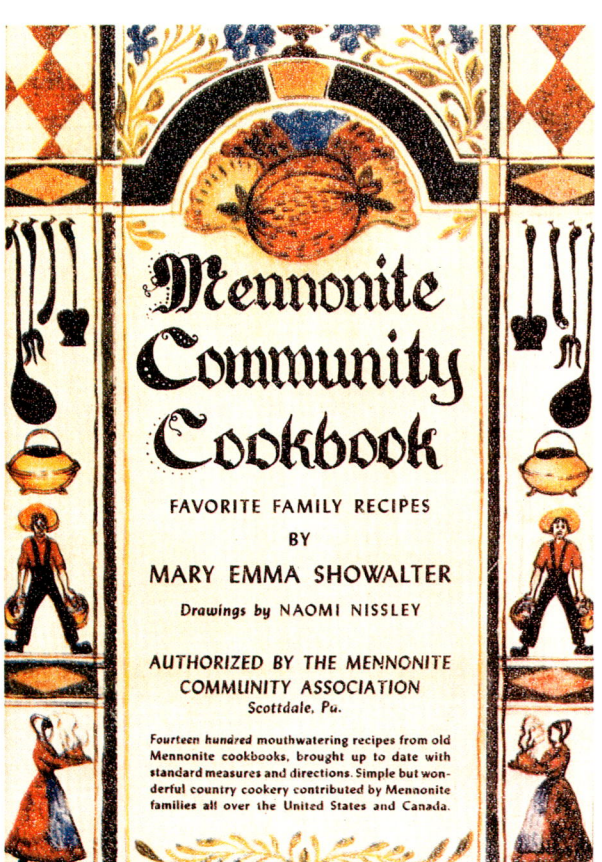

One of the more desirable American cookbooks is "La Cuisine Creole," devoted to New Orleans dishes. It was compiled in 1885 by Lafcadio Hearn, noted for writings on the Far East. A first edition sold for $850 in 1977.

A religious-community book that was put out for the Mennonites has 1,400 family recipes as well as a menu designed for a meal to be served at a barn-raising.

Commercial cookbooks, distributed free or for a small charge, are attractive as mementos and useful as sources of recipes. This one was issued in 1913 to push a then-new shortening, naturally used in all the recipes.

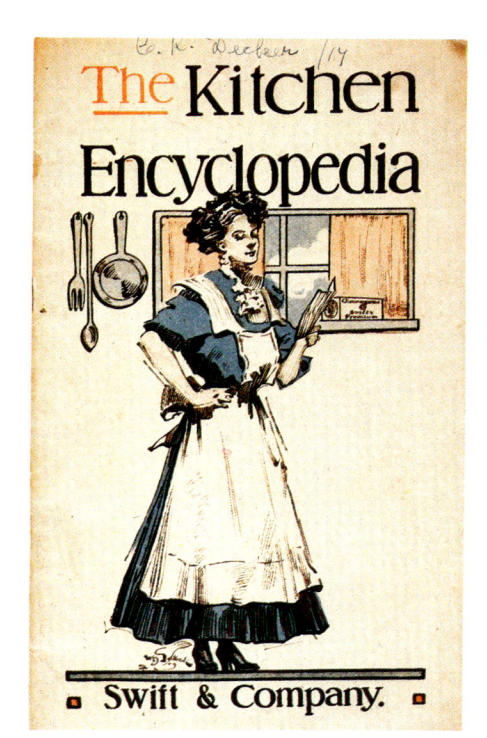

COOKBOOKS / 15

In a 1911 book given away by a meat packer, recipes called for the firm's margarine, visible on the window sill in the cover illustration.

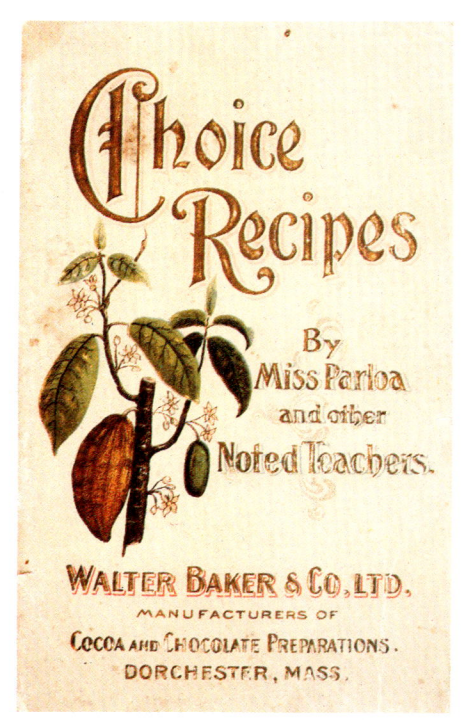

Recipes by Maria Parloa, founder of the Boston Cooking School made famous by Fannie Farmer, were published by a cocoa maker.

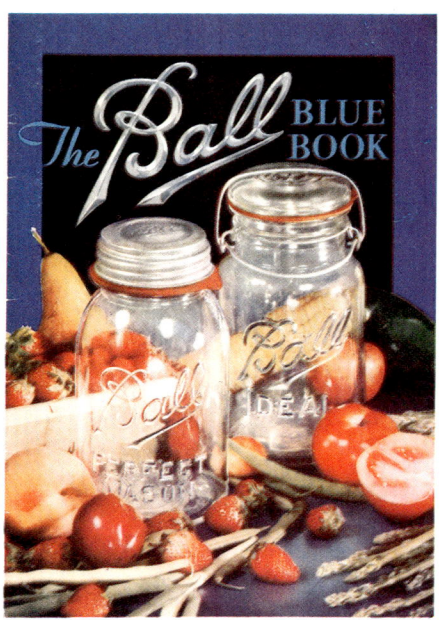

This slightly dog-eared copy of a preserving guide, offered over many decades by a jar manufacturer, is a rare 1932 edition.

Shrimp Supreme

Here's a casserole that can be made ahead of time and then baked just before serving.

- 1 pound large raw shrimp, fresh or frozen
- 1 tablespoon Chicken Seasoned Stock Base
- 1 cup hot water
- ½ cup rice
- ¼ cup butter
- 1 tablespoon Arrowroot
- 1½ cups milk
- ½ teaspoon Dill Weed
- 1 tablespoon Eschalot Wine Vinegar
- 1 teaspoon Beau Monde Seasoning
- ½ teaspoon salt
- 1½ cups shredded Cheddar cheese
- Paprika

Shell and devein shrimp. Dissolve Chicken Seasoned Stock Base in hot water; bring to a boil, add rice. Turn down heat, cover and steam until rice is done. Melt butter; remove from heat and stir in Arrowroot. Add milk; return to heat and cook, stirring constantly, until thickened and smooth. Stir in Dill Weed, Vinegar, Beau Monde, and salt. Add cleaned shrimp and simmer gently for about 10 minutes or until shrimp turn red. Spoon rice into a buttered 1½-quart baking dish. Pour shrimp over rice; top with shredded cheese and sprinkle with Paprika. Bake in a 350° oven for 25 to 30 minutes or until cheese is melted and rice and shrimp are hot. Serve hot. Makes 6 servings.

Bombay Shrimp Curry

Apples and Onions simmered and then puréed give this curry sauce its interesting flavor and consistency. Serve with steamed or boiled rice.

- 1 pound large raw shrimp
- ¼ cup butter
- 1 tablespoon Curry Powder
- 4 tablespoons Instant Minced Onions
- 4 tablespoons water
- 3 medium-size apples, peeled and sliced, or 1½ cups drained canned apples
- 2 cups hot water
- 1 tablespoon Chicken Seasoned Stock Base
- 1 tablespoon Beau Monde Seasoning
- 2 teaspoons Arrowroot
- 1 tablespoon cold water
- 3 hard-cooked eggs
- ¼ cup undiluted evaporated milk

Shell and devein shrimp. Melt butter; stir in Curry Powder and cook for 3 or 4 minutes over low heat. Meanwhile, rehydrate Onions in water; add to Curry and simmer for 2 or 3 minutes. Add apples, hot water, Chicken Seasoned Stock Base, and Beau Monde. Simmer gently for about 40 minutes, stirring occasionally. Put through food mill or wire sieve. Add shrimp to Curry Sauce and simmer for 30 minutes. Mix Arrowroot and cold water and stir into sauce. Cook until thickened. Slice hard-cooked eggs; add to Curry along with milk. Serve hot. Makes 6 servings.

78 SEAFOOD

A purveyor of spices and seasonings compiled "The Spice Islands Cook Book" (above) in 1961. Illustrated with watercolors of flowers and spice-producing plants, it was not given away but was sold in bookstores.

THE ALICE B. TOKLAS COOK BOOK

ILLUSTRATIONS BY
SIR FRANCIS ROSE

Harper & Brothers NEW YORK

Personal fame adds as much as quality of the food to the desirability of "celebrity" cookbooks like this one, which devotes a third of its space to reminiscences of the author's life with poet Gertrude Stein in Paris in the 1920s and 1930s.

A photo of dancer Margot Fonteyn accompanies her recipe for veal scallops in "The Ballet Cook Book" by Tanaquil Le Clercq, ballerina.

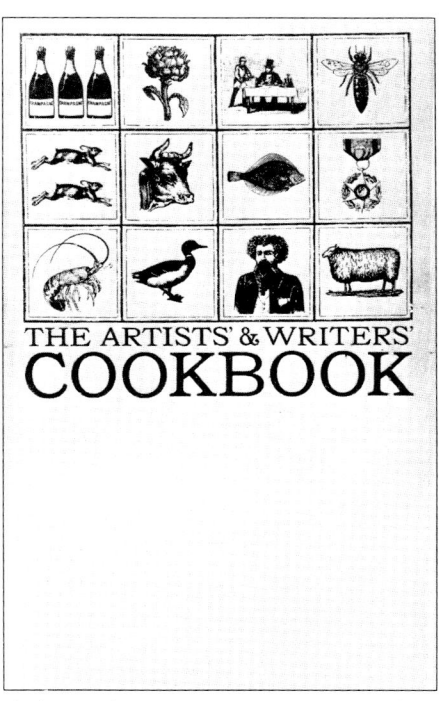

Artists and writers past and present, from John Keats to Lillian Hellman, provided the recipes and menus offered in this 1961 book.

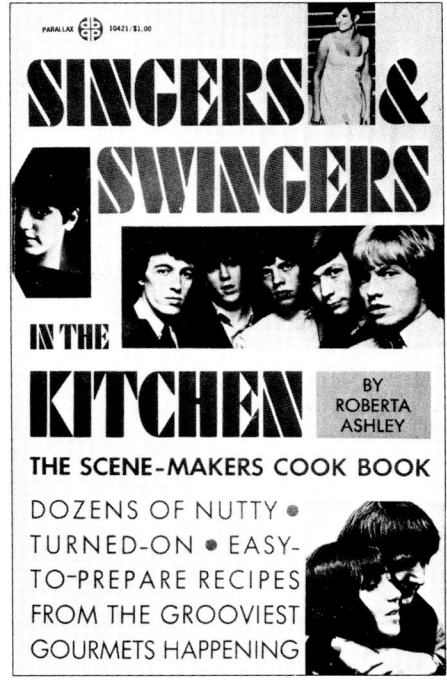

Singer Barbra Streisand (top) and Mick Jagger (center in group) are among those who suggested recipes for this 1967 book.

COOKBOOKS / 17

Delectable Writing About Food

No cookbook collector worth his salt and pepper would ignore books about food simply because they are not collections of recipes. The layout of a kitchen *(right)*, the history of national and ethnic cooking and eating patterns—these are only a small number of the many culinary subjects that have been examined assiduously by outstanding writers.

Several of the books that discuss cooking rather than try to teach it are desirable because they are comprehensive reference works. But others are sought for the authority, wisdom or wit their authors apply to an endeavor that is not often subjected to intellectual scrutiny.

An 1870 kitchen layout in "American Heritage Cookbook" is taken from "Principles of Domestic Science"—by Catharine E. Beecher and her sister Harriet Beecher Stowe, famous for "Uncle Tom's Cabin."

The frontispiece above is from Anthelme Brillat-Savarin's philosophical analysis of 1826, "The Physiology of Taste."

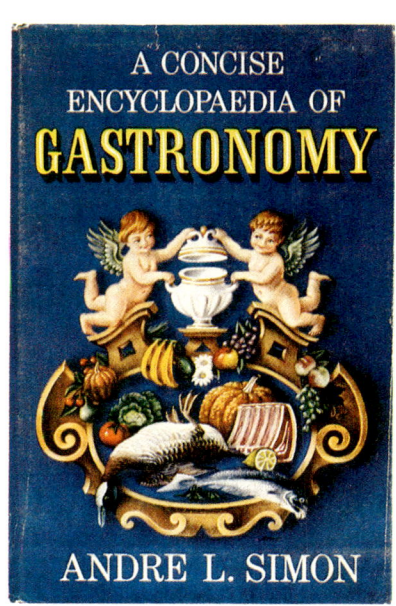

Andre Simon's "A Concise Encyclopaedia of Gastronomy" (1939) is considered by many the classic modern reference.

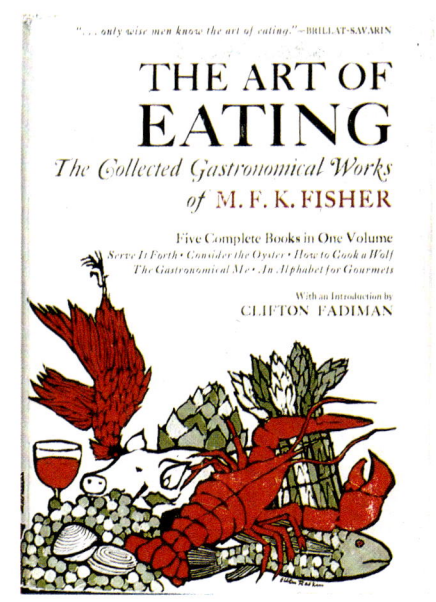

In this anthology of articles, M. F. K. Fisher comments wittily on the civilized subjects of cooking, eating, good conversation and love.

18 / COOKBOOKS

James Beard's 1960 "Treasury of Outdoor Cooking" includes a menu for a Hawaiian luau that is illustrated by a reproduction of a Gauguin painting.

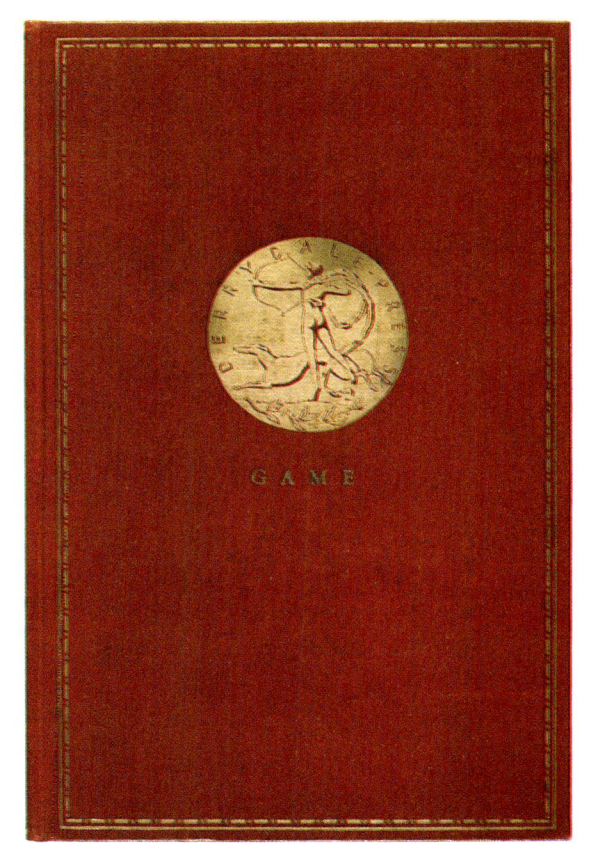

Among cookbooks that are collectible because their focus is unique is Elizabeth O. Hiller's, published in 1918. It has a different salad for every day of the year, including not only such familiar dishes as hot potato salad but also one that uses marshmallows.

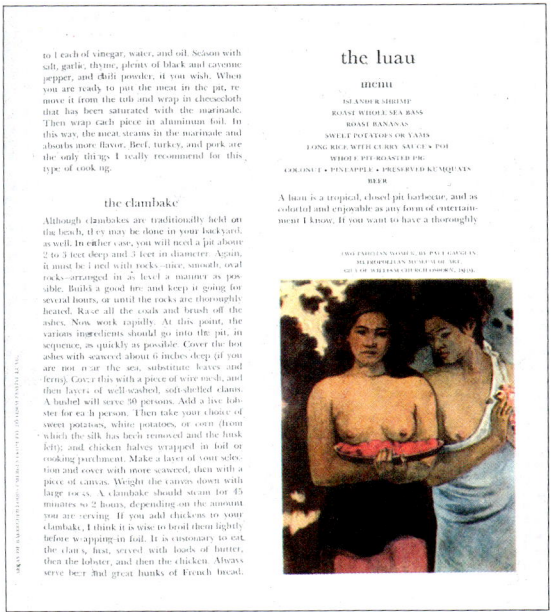

Two volumes, one on fish and one on game, by L. P. de Gouy were issued in a limited edition in 1937. Several decades later the value of a copy was well over $100.

"Pastry Making Is Child's Play," claims the French title of Michel Oliver's 1966 collection of dessert recipes for children in French and English. It offers child-pleasers like chocolate truffles and marble cake.

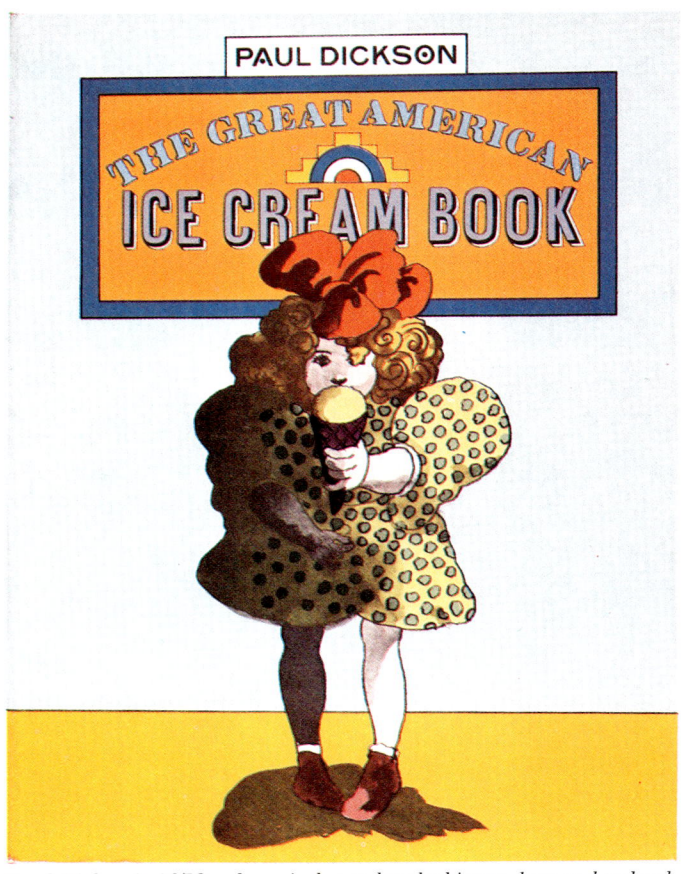

Paul Dickson's 1972 volume is devoted to the history, lore and technology of ice-cream making. Included are recipes for making such little-known concoctions as the Panama cooler.

LIBRARIES

American Antiquarian Society
Worcester, Massachusetts 01609

Katherine Golden Bitting Gastronomic Library
The Rare Book and Special Collections Division
Library of Congress
Washington, D.C. 20540

California Cookbooks Collection
Department of Special Collections
University Research Library
University of California at Los Angeles
Los Angeles, California 90024

Cleveland Public Library
Cleveland, Ohio 44114

New York Public Library
New York, New York 10018

Schlesinger Library
Radcliffe College
Cambridge, Massachusetts 02138

BOOKS

Axford, Lavonne Brady, ed., *English Language Cookbooks, 1600-1973*. Gale Research Company, 1976.

Bitting, Katherine Golden, *Gastronomic Bibliography*. Gryphon Books, 1971.

Brown, Eleanor and Bob, *Culinary Americana, 100 Years of Cookbooks Published in the United States from 1860-1960*. Roving Eye Press, 1961.

Hess, John L. and Karen, *The Taste of America*. Grossman Publishers, 1977.

Lowenstein, Eleanor, *Bibliography of American Cookery Books 1742-1860*. American Antiquarian Society and Corner Book Shop, 1972.

Patten, Marguerite, *Books for Cooks, A Bibliography of Cookery*. Bowker Publishing Company, 1975.

Tannahill, Reay, *Food In History*. Stein and Day Publishers, 1973.

Corkscrews
An Armory of Gear to Open the Wine

Sometime in the 17th Century an ingenious vintner thought to seal his bottles with corks, thus preventing airborne organisms from souring the wine and enabling it to mature in flavor as it aged. His invention created the necessity for the invention of the corkscrew by another unknown.

Soon corkscrews were available, if unusual. A 1700 issue of the literary magazine *The London Spy* ran an account of a dinner party at which the host presented a corked bottle of wine and asked "But what shall we do with it? We cannot open it." The day, or evening, was saved by a parson, according to the magazine. Said he, "I believe I may have a little engine in my pocket that may unlock the difficulty." Since then hundreds of little engines have been dreamed up to uncork bottles.

Wine corks must fit tightly into the bottle and, dampened by the wine, they adhere to the glass. To break this adhesion and pull the cork takes an effort estimated to be the equivalent of lifting a 100-pound bag of cement. So corkscrews use various devices to maximize the force: levers, screws, curved gears and rack-and-pinion gears.

Some of these contrivances do the job well. Others appear to have been designed chiefly to astonish the beholder with their ingenuity and dismay the user with their inutility. Both varieties are prized by collectors. I know an engineer in Sweden who was delighted when I sent him a corkscrew that had no fewer than 75 parts. A

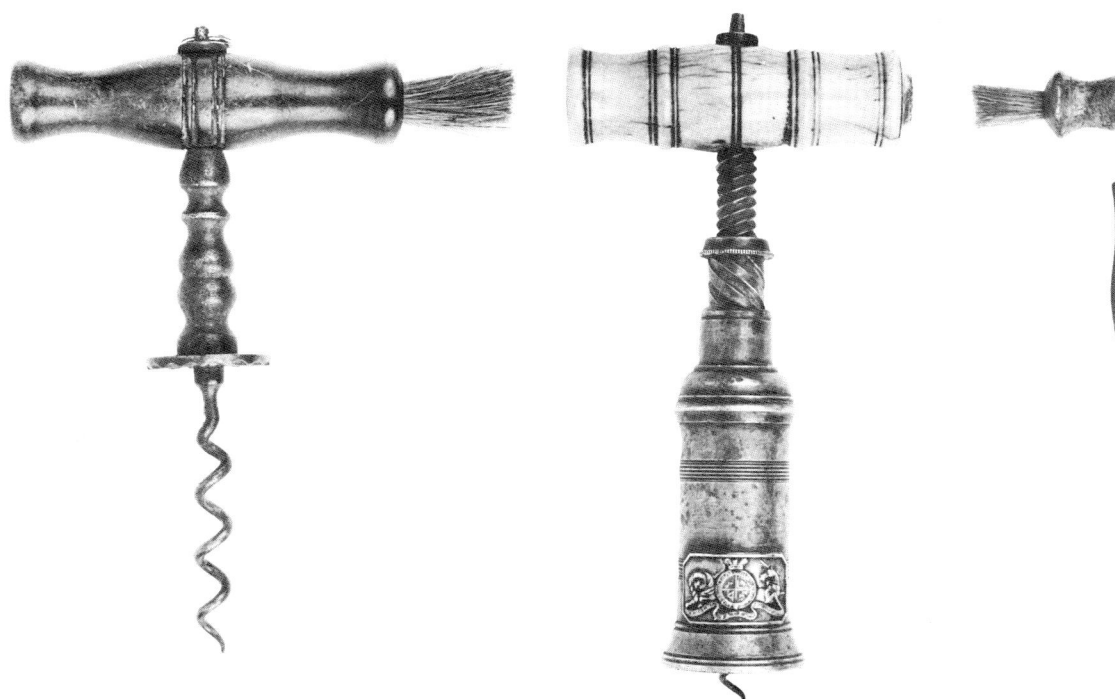

Brother Timothy Diener is cellarmaster of Mont La Salle Vineyards, near Napa, California, which are operated by The Christian Brothers, a teaching order of the Roman Catholic Church.

Samuel Henshall's corkscrew, the first to win an English patent, in 1795, is equipped with a brush to dust the label and cork.

The barrel of Edward Thomason's invention, patented 1802, centered the screw and, resting on the bottle lip, provided leverage.

The London Rack, patented by William Lund in 1855, has one handle for the screw and one with rack-and-pinion gearing to lift the cork.

Brother Timothy Diener uses a wart-hog-tusk corkscrew similar to the one on page 24, to uncork a bottle from the vineyard he oversees as cellarmaster.

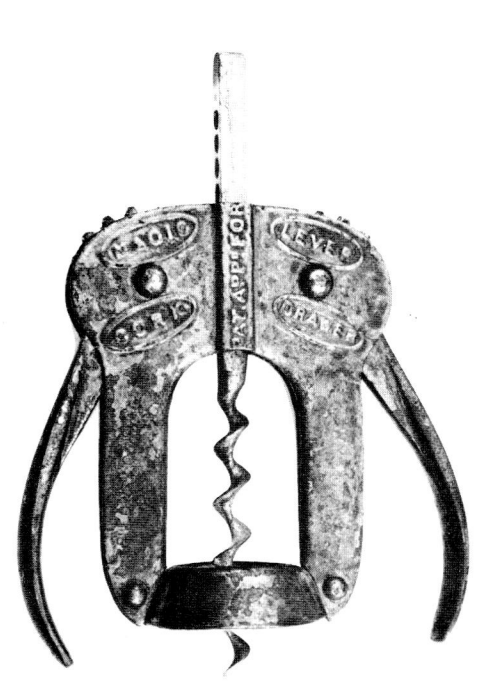

The Magic Lever Cork Drawer—a type now common—inserts the screw as gears raise the levers. Depressing the levers lifts the cork.

Pins of the U-Neek are meant to be pushed into the cork individually. Then the whole device is turned to twist the cork out.

On this German model, handles and shaft turn together to insert the screw. After the handles touch the frame they lift shaft and cork.

man in Connecticut specializes in worthless models—the less useful the corkscrew the more collectible it is to him.

A more mundane avenue of specialization is to collect according to the material or decoration of the handle. Naturally, precious materials and outstanding workmanship add to value. But age is important. While unusual examples from recent times—such as Old Snifter *(page 27)*—are desirable, many made after the latter part of the 19th Century were mass-produced and are too common to intrigue collectors.

One clue to age may be brand name and patent date, marked on many of the devices. Among the most valuable examples are a Henshall's *(page 20)*, marked with the name and the motto *Obstando Promoves* (to make advancement by standing firm), and a Hull's Royal Club *(opposite)* bearing a patent "seal"—a soldered-on decorative emblem seldom used after the middle of the 19th Century. By the mid-1970s, the Royal Club was worth about $300 at auction. The patent date is not proof of age, however, for some mechanisms, such as Lund's London Rack *(page 20)*, were made with stamped dates over many decades. You must judge workmanship, wear marks and patina to identify the old.

As desirable as antiquity is distinctive design. Corkscrews lend themselves to making up part of a combination tool. Some bespeak the good, or at least the more luxurious, life: a corkscrew combined with a cigar cutter, or with a brush to remove dust and cobwebs from bottles of very old vintages. Other combinations are baffling: a corkscrew with a glass cutter, or with a cigarette-making machine, knife, buttonhook and screwdriver.

To identify a particular find and thus establish its age and possible rarity, serious collectors study patent records—particularly British ones. Some details from their research have been summarized, with illustrations, in magazine articles such as "Corkscrews," by Charles R. Beard, in *The Connoisseur* for July-December 1929, and "Collecting Corkscrews" by Homer Babbidge, in *Americana* for May-June 1977. Although a 1929 magazine is a collector's item itself, copies can be found in large libraries; or for a fee, ordered in photocopy form by your local librarian through an interlibrary loan service.

Though antique shops abroad, especially in London, offer the best chances for finding rare corkscrews, unusual ones turn up anywhere. Some years ago in a California shop I acquired for $10 a corkscrew with a handle of wart-hog tusk, its end tipped with a silver cigar cutter *(page 24)*—as far as I know it is the only one of its kind.

There is an organization of corkscrew collectors, but, as is suggested by its name—the International Correspondence of Corkscrew Addicts—it does not take itself solemnly. It limits its membership to 50 and has no president, only a "Right," a designation selected to honor Kentucky Congressman Henry Clay, who said, "I would rather be right than President." I was ICCA's first Right and when I left office, I became the Just Right.

CORKSCREWS / 23

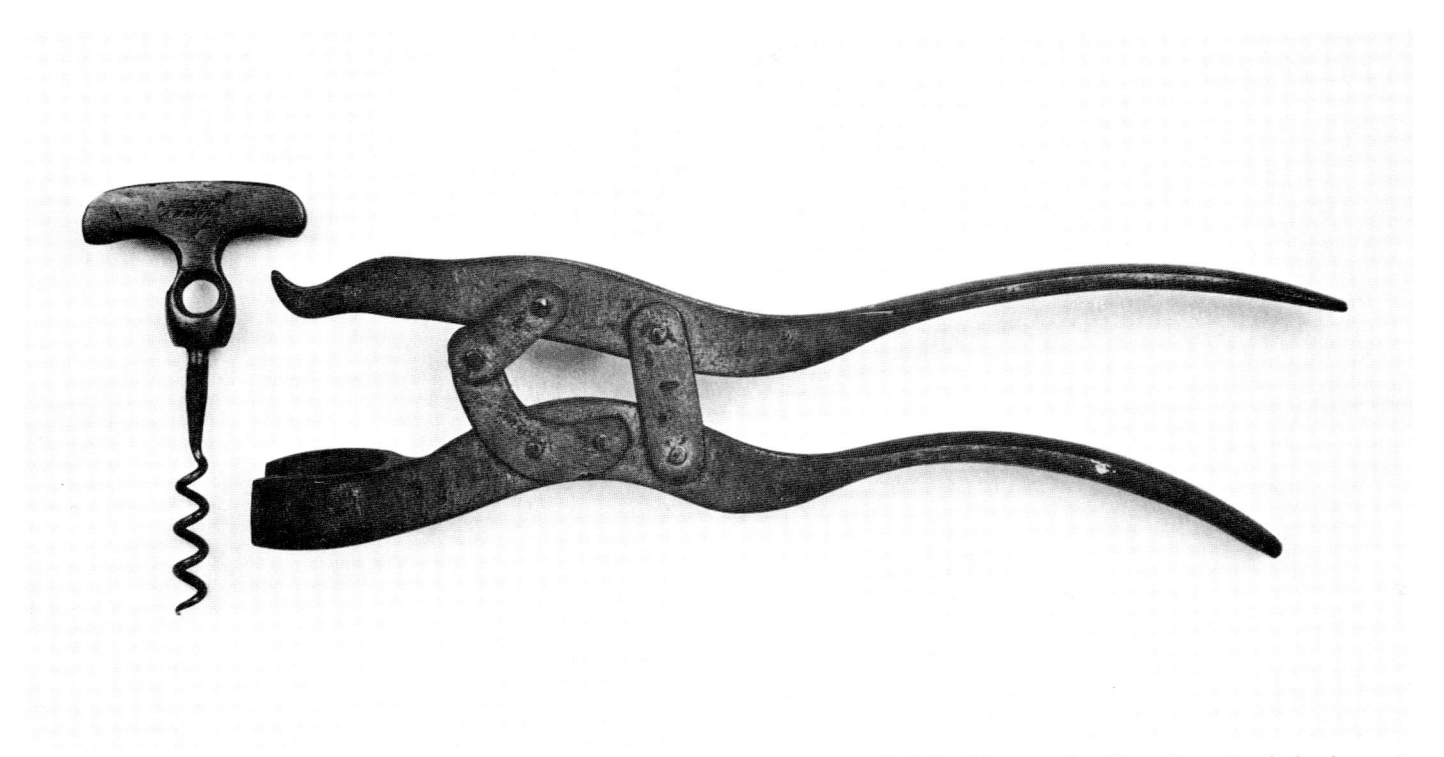

This type of two-part corkscrew is rare. With the screw inserted, the pincers lift it by hooking the hole of the screw handle and pressing the bottle mouth.

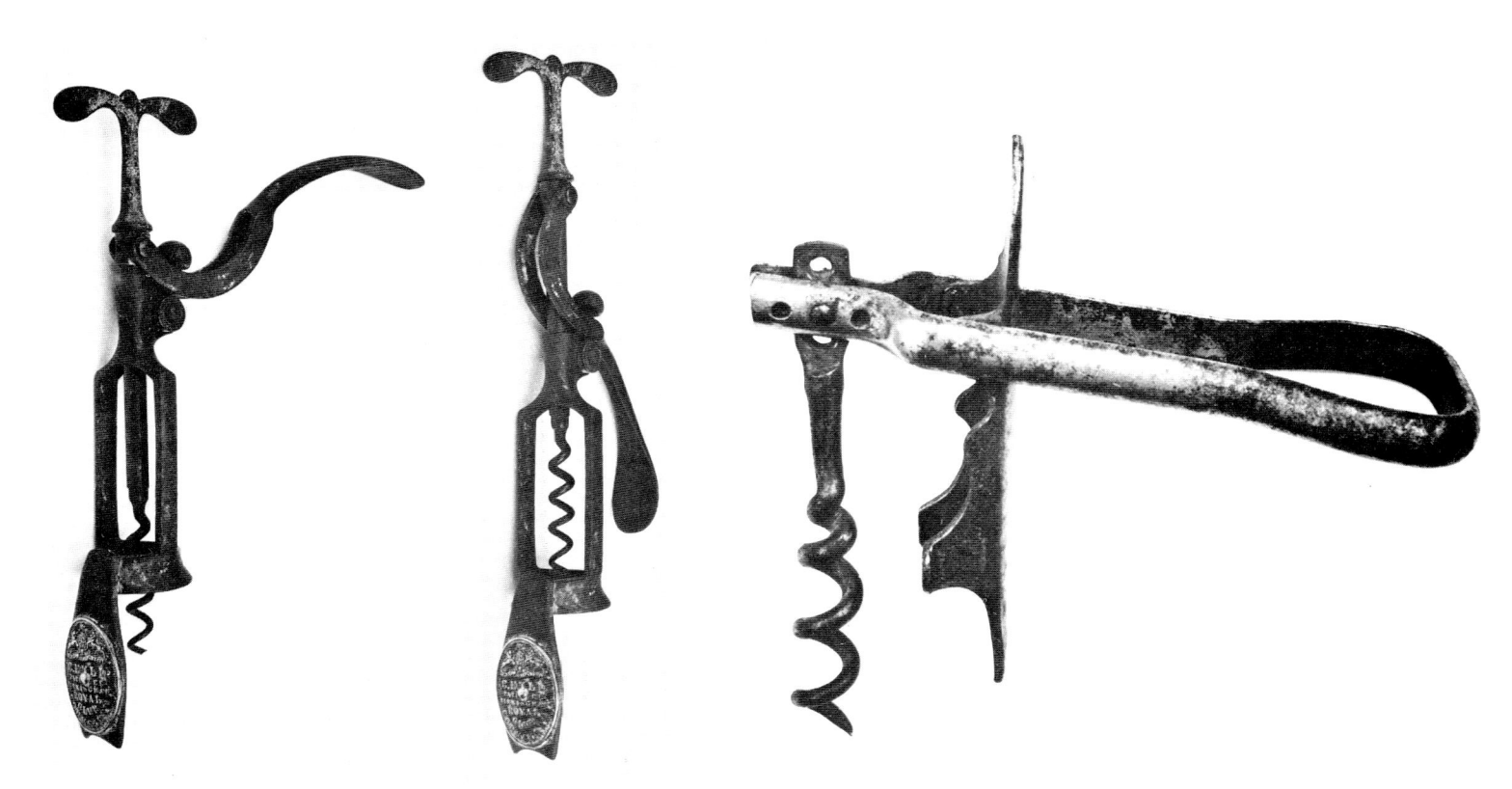

The Royal Club, patented by Charles Hull in 1864, has a pumplike handle that is depressed (above, right) to lift the cork. This example's 1864 patent seal, soldered to the bottom, adds value.

An American folding corkscrew of the 19th Century is similar to ones used today by waiters, but has the hooked fulcrum behind the screw, not in front—the handle must be pressed down rather than raised.

24 / CORKSCREWS

This rustic French corkscrew is prized for its appropriate handle, which was taken from a piece of an old grapevine. It measures 14 inches across.

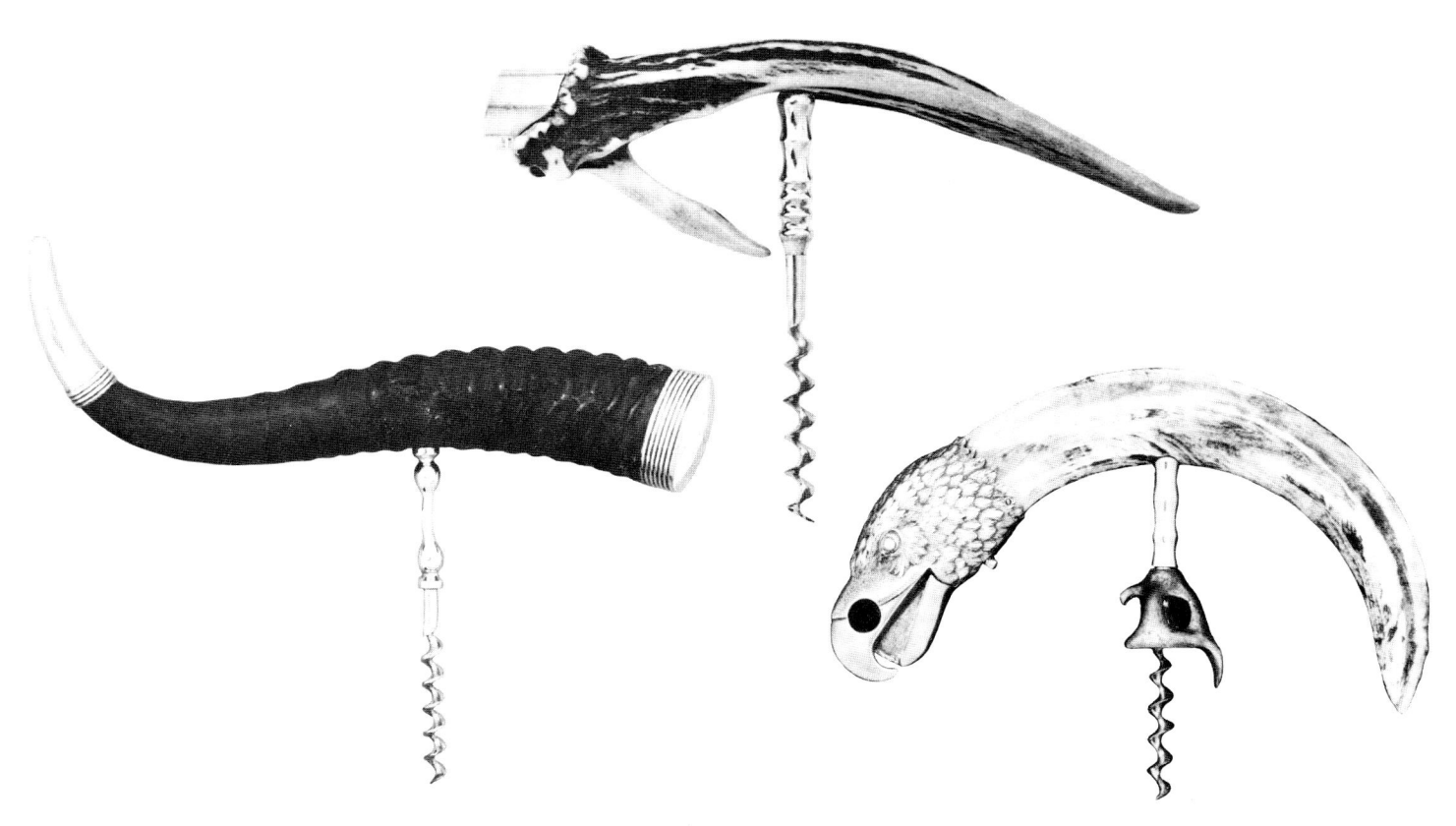

Animal horn and tusks have been favorite materials for corkscrew handles, and examples like these are valued because the design or the animal is unusual. At left is an antelope horn with silver ends. The staghorn handle in the center includes the part of the horn that protected the stag's eye. This corkscrew is at least 50 years old. At right is a curved wart-hog tusk; the eagle's beak is a cigar cutter, the hook near the screw a cap lifter.

Special Pullers for Special Stoppers

Until metal caps came into general use in the 20th Century, not only wine but many other liquids, like perfume, medicine and soft drinks, were sold in containers that were sealed with corks. Corkscrews were fashioned to suit all of them, and make up a category that attracts collectors.

A number of these specialized corkscrews are miniatures, like the advertising premiums at right—either because the containers were normally correspondingly small or because the pullers were meant to be kept handy in a pocket or purse. Others, such as the perfume-bottle corkscrew at bottom, right, are as large as the devices designed for wines and are handsomely fitted with costly handles. Almost all, however, are mechanically simple; since less effort is required to pull a perfume-bottle stopper than a wine cork, there was no need for the gears and levers that were devised to ease the task of opening a tightly sealed wine bottle.

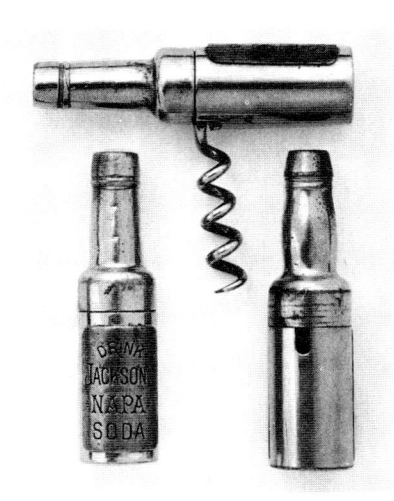

The small folding corkscrews at left, in the shape of soft-drink bottles, were giveaways for Jackson Napa soda, a mineral water.

Some miniatures were simply twisted wire (above, right); the one at left has a ring guard to prevent snagging in a purse.

This perfume-bottle corkscrew, 5 inches long, has a handle made of mother-of-pearl and was meant to be kept on a lady's dressing table.

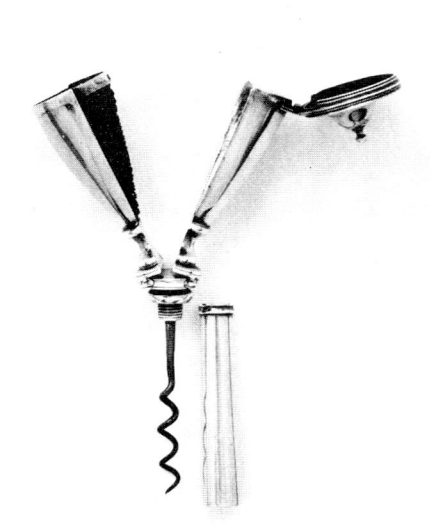

An 1806 hallmarked silver corkscrew has a sheath and, for a handle, a capped nutmeg holder and a grater—to make mulled wine.

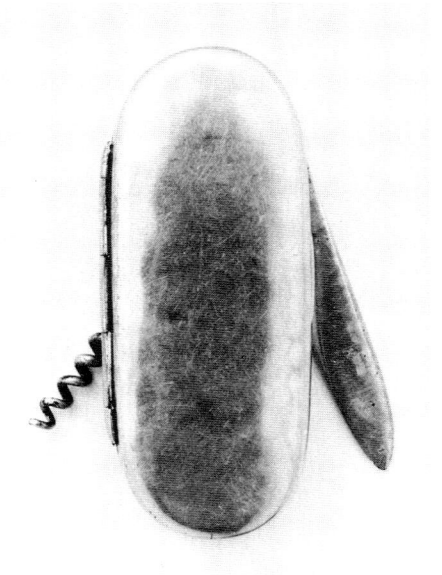

A silver-plated snuffbox, Scandinavian in origin and dating from 1900, incorporates a foldaway corkscrew and knife blade.

A cork puller handed out by the C. D. Kenny Coffee Company could pry off bottle caps with the loop at the right end of the handle.

26 / CORKSCREWS

Two of these bar accessories—the French swan (its screw sheathed) and the rhino from Peru—are solid silver. The English horse is silver-plated.

These animal-handled corkscrews, photographed inserted into the bottle corks, are typical of the recently made novelties that appeal to many collectors.

Old Snifter, a combination corkscrew and bottle opener, is supposed to be a caricature of Congressman Andrew Volstead, who was author of the federal law that enforced Prohibition between 1919 and 1933.

Tongs for Port

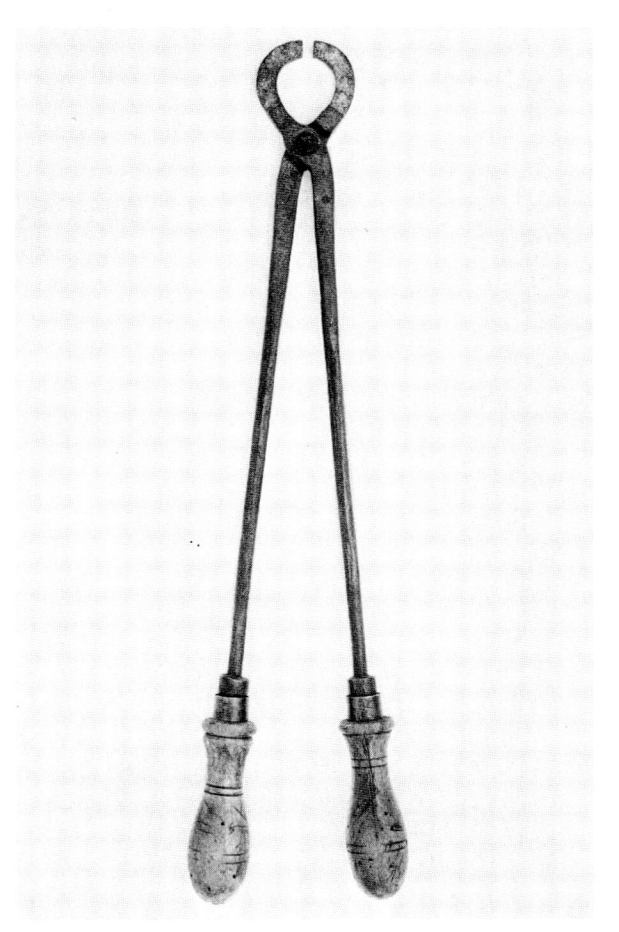

Very old bottles of the sweet, strong wine called port acquire a coating of pigment that would be shaken into the wine if a corkscrew were used. Instead, tongs like these are heated red-hot, then applied to the bottle neck, which cracks away neatly when a wet cloth is wrapped around it.

MUSEUM
The Wine Museum of San Francisco
San Francisco, California 94109

BOOKS
Adams, Leon D., *Leon D. Adams' Commonsense Book of Wine.* Houghton Mifflin Company, 1975.

Amerine, Maynard A., and V. Singleton, *Wine, An Introduction for Americans.* University of California Press, 1965.

LOG CABIN SONGS
BY JOHNNY CROCKETT

WITH GUITAR CHORDS

CROCKETT KENTUCKY MOUNTAINEERS
FATHER CROCKETT & FIVE SONS

PRICE 50¢ NET

MADE IN USA

GOODMAN MUSIC CO.
MUSIC PUBLISHERS
New York, N.Y.

Country Music
The Oldtime Sound Preserved

*My good gal's trying to make a fool out of me,
Trying to make me believe that I ain't got that old T.B.*

To me, Jimmie Rodgers singing those words from his song "T.B. Blues" is what country music is all about. I instantly became a collector when I first heard his records on the radio. I went out and tried to buy them, but the stores had none. This was 1948. Rodgers, a star of the late 1920s and early 1930s, had been dead—of that old T.B.—for 15 years.

I figured that if the stores did not stock the records, maybe the people who had bought them years before would still have them. I went calling on people in my hometown, Frederick, Maryland—always to the back door of the house, where friends and family were expected—to ask just as politely as I knew how if they had

Joseph E. Bussard Jr. broadcasts examples from his collection of some 20,000 country-music records on WELD, in Fisher, West Virginia.

any old Jimmie Rodgers records that they did not want. I soon learned that "No, we don't, Joe" meant just that, whereas "Not today" meant, "Yes, but we don't want to sell them, at least not right now."

When I had exhausted Frederick, I began to search the countryside. At 16 I got my first car, and that beat-up Chevy opened up practically the whole South to me. Many a time I drove down roads so curvy that I wore out my horn, as the saying goes, blowing at my own taillights. I got to know exactly when to drive on by and when to stop. I stopped if I saw a house with not too much paint on it, with old-fashioned latticework, maybe a stained-glass window in the door or a lace curtain. To me that house just hollered, "Old records! Come on in!" One Virginia road had just five houses on it; every one of them had good records. In one, a woman brought out a stack 2 feet high. When I asked how much, she said, "Just take 'em." There was a Jimmie Rodgers in mint condition in that stack.

Father Johnny Crockett, better known as Dad, sits at far left in this stagy photograph for a songbook cover. His Kentucky Mountaineers recorded such typical country music as "Shoo Fly" and "The Hard Cider Song" for Crown and Brunswick records, now rare, in the 1920s and 1930s.

Since I began driving mountain roads in that Chevy, many people have joined me in collecting everything connected with country music: song sheets and songbooks, advertising fliers, photographs, catalogues, posters and—best of all, because I can play them—the old records themselves.

The subject is difficult to define, for it takes in different kinds of music with different names *(box, page 30)*. But there's a common thread. All country music was written by rural Americans for their own kind of people. Recordings of these songs multiplied abruptly in the 1920s, dwindled during the Depression, then revived after World War II in a more commercialized form. The history is complicated by the mixing of the musical traditions of mountains, bayous and plains, of whites and blacks, of cowboys, farmers, railroad men and miners. Records and memorabilia recalling landmarks or identifying notable figures in this complex history—especially from the early days—are what collectors seek.

Country music was strongly influenced by so-called race records: blues songs performed by blacks for a black audience. Some were jazz, "city blues" by such artists as Mamie Smith and the legendary Bessie Smith, backed up by piano or small bands. Others were country blues sung, to a guitar accompaniment, by the likes of Papa Charlie Jackson and Blind Lemon Jefferson.

Country music by white artists, as distinguished from race records, first appeared in quantity on records bearing the OKeh label. By 1923 the company had considerable experience in marketing race records under the direction of a producer named Ralph Peer. Its top retailer in this line was Polk Brockman, who did his selling in a corner of his grandfather's furniture emporium in Atlanta. During a business trip to New York, he went to the movies; the show included a newsreel with scenes of a fiddlers' contest in the South, which gave Brockman an idea. He called on Peer to say that he believed there was a market for white country music as well as black.

Within a short time Peer arrived in Atlanta, accompanied by two sound engineers and a load of recording equipment. Brockman had already picked out a local country artist: Fiddlin' John Carson, a sometime jockey, millworker, moonshiner and house painter who played whenever he could find listeners. He was a familiar fig-

A MUSICAL BLEND OF AFRICA AND EUROPE

To some people country music is Elizabethan folk songs performed outside cabins in Appalachia; to others it is cowboy laments; to still others it is blues crooned by a black woman. It is all those things — and several others — because many related forms of this American art arose from the same origins.

Country music comes from two distinct musical traditions, one white, one black. The white strain is the Anglo-Celtic folk song, brought to the rural South in colonial days and preserved there.

The black strain came with the Africans brought to America as slaves and was retained by them in chants, work songs and gospel singing. All country music is about rural American life. The songs speak of love, of troubles with hard times and alcohol, of faith in religion and family ties, of the exploits and bad ends of outlaws.

Associated with country music are several terms, some of which are different names for country music while others define related forms of music. Among the terms most often encountered are:

BLUEGRASS: Played by bands—generally consisting of fiddle, guitar, mandolin, string bass and banjo—with a strong, syncopated beat, and at breakneck speed

CAJUN: Songs with a strong infusion of the folk music of the French bayou country, such as "Jambalaya" performed by Hank Williams

CITY BLUES: A precursor of jazz, exemplified by Mamie Smith's singing with orchestral or piano accompaniment

COUNTRY-AND-WESTERN: Commercialized songs that deal with country-music themes, with elaborate accompaniment

COUNTRY BLUES: Black music that retains its rural atmosphere, most often sung with guitar accompaniment

COUNTRY SWING: A lively, danceable hybrid of country music and big-band dance music that originated in Texas and Oklahoma in the early 1930s. Also called Western swing

COWBOY MUSIC: Country music with Western or cowboy themes, first sung by cowboys. Also called Western music

HILLBILLY MUSIC: Derogatory term for country music

HONKY-TONK: Played by bands—usually fiddle, guitars, bass and drums—for dancing in roadhouses

MOUNTAIN MUSIC: Country music

OLD-TIME MUSIC: Genteel term for country music

RACE RECORDS: Euphemism coined in the 1920s by recording companies and generally applied to all recorded performances by black artists

Some of the rarest of all country blues were released on Black Patti Records by such artists as Long Cleve Reed. Black Patti, founded in March 1927, folded six months later, having issued 55 releases. Many of its records have been priced at hundreds of dollars.

Blind Lemon Jefferson is regarded by jazz and country-music collectors as one of the greatest early blues singers. He recorded 100 songs between 1925 and his death in 1930. This record with his picture on the label — a rare tribute — was issued by Paramount in 1928 for his birthday.

Like most of the large recording companies in the 1920s, Victor advertised black country music in separate catalogues known as race catalogues. In this case the word "race" did not appear on the cover, but the illustration clearly indicates the kind of recordings listed and the audiences for which they were made. Sermons by black ministers and novelties—comedy dialogues—were included with the musical recordings.

A Victor flier of the late 1920s lists songs by the first important jug band to make records. A jug band usually included string instruments plus a jug played by blowing across its mouth.

A 1936 flier lists hillbilly music and songs by black artists recorded on the Blue Bird label, which Victor launched during the Depression for low-priced recordings of popular music.

OKeh's landmark 1923 recording of two songs by Fiddlin' John Carson was a quick success. Though not the first country-music recording by a white artist, it established country music as popular entertainment.

ure at Georgia political rallies and a regular performer on Atlanta radio station WSB. On June 14, 1923, Peer recorded "The Old Hen Cackled and The Rooster's Going To Crow" and, on the other side, "The Little Old Log Cabin in the Lane." Peer hated the music but must have liked the sales: 500 copies the first month.

Other record companies were now quick to get into what they could see would be a new market. Like Peer, their representatives went out into the field to look for talent and record it. A few of the record companies' discoveries were brought to New York or Chicago to record. The majority, however, sang or played in temporary studios—converted barns, warehouses and hotel rooms. It was cheap to make records then. Artists were paid little (often a flat $50, and no royalties), so producers would cheerfully take a chance on anybody, black or white, who could walk, hitch or pay the train fare to wherever the company had set up camp.

In Georgia, Columbia Records representatives found Riley Puckett, a blind street singer and guitarist, and Gid Tanner, chicken farmer and fiddler. In Tennessee, a producer for the Vocalion label found Uncle Am Stuart, another fiddler. In Illinois, the Gennett label was enriched by the voice of Bradley Kincaid, a Kentucky mountain boy working his way through college by singing country music on WLS radio in Chicago, where many poor Southerners had migrated to find work. Victor found cowboy singer Carl T. Sprague in Texas, and another performer from Texas on its own doorstep.

This was Vernon Dalhart, a versatile, ambitious singer who was recording light opera in New York. Dalhart begged for the chance to record some country songs, hoping, no doubt, for a bigger audience. He got it with Victor's release of a song Dalhart had previously recorded for Edison: "The Wreck of the Old 97." Sales of that ballad about a famous train crash, with "The Prisoner's Song" on the other side, ultimately topped a million. Dalhart, who recorded for any company that would hire him, used a variety of pseudonyms: Al Craver, Frank Evans and Will Terry, as well as Dalhart, which itself was a pseudonym—for Marion Slaughter.

Among the singers discovered by the wide-ranging recording crews was Jimmie Rodgers. The son of a railroad man, raised in railside shanties and freight-yard shacks, he too was working on the railroad by the time he was 14. Everywhere he traveled, he heard the country music that was being sung in the area and met the people to whom the music was a way of life. An important factor in his career, one that was to contribute heavily to his style of singing country blues, was the many years he spent with blacks. And he developed his own version of the yodel, swinging into falsetto in the manner of Swiss and other Alpine folk singers.

By 1927, tuberculosis had forced Rodgers to retire from the railroad, and he was trying to support his family by singing. He went to the Victor auditions in Bristol, Tennessee. I would have loved to have been there to watch and listen as Rodgers sang, drawing from his time on the railroad, from the singing styles of the blacks he had worked with, the other traditions he had absorbed, and his own and others' misfortunes and heartaches.

Ralph Peer, who had by this time moved from OKeh to Victor, was running Victor's audition sessions there in Bristol, and he liked what he heard: "The Soldier's Sweetheart." The public liked it, too. Recording followed recording, and Jimmie Rodgers became the first national star of country music.

The audition call that brought Jimmie Rodgers also attracted, two days later, the Carter Family. They were to provide another strand of country music—the almost austere religious sound that Maybelle, Sara and her husband, known as A. P., had grown up with in Appalachia. Their recording of "Wandering Boy" made them, like Rodgers, national stars.

The Carter and Rodgers records were among the first made electrically, which provided sound quality vastly superior to the old mechanical method, and this helped their sales. But when the Depression hit in 1929, it hit country music with devastating force; little recording

COUNTRY MUSIC / 33

Earl Johnson, flanked by the Clodhoppers, his brothers Albert (banjo) and Ester (guitar), was one of Georgia's best "breakdown" fiddlers. The breakdown — the record at right is one — is a tune played extremely fast.

The word "electric" on this 1927 label indicates that the recording was produced by the then-new process using electric equipment instead of the old mechanical method. By 1930, all records were produced electrically.

In the early 1930s few records were pressed and fewer sold, so Luke Highnight and His Ozark Strutters were lucky to record "Sailing on the Ocean" for Vocalion. Today the record is rare.

Brunswick issued records with its own label as well as the Vocalion, Silvertone (for Sears) and Melotone labels. The record shown here is a 1931 issue, rare because few were made in that Depression year.

was done. A revival came only after World War II. In the years following I bought lots of records, but I found that country music was moribund. Imitators of Jimmie Rodgers abounded. Performers only repeated what they heard on the radio and on jukeboxes. One notable exception was Hank Williams. Composer, lyricist and singer, he, like Rodgers, drew on his own experiences in an original way. Other exceptions were the artists who played bluegrass music, a fresh, relatively pure form of country music that still continues.

Hank Williams died in 1953—and 1953 is the cutoff point for my collection. I do not feel deprived, for even with the gap of the Depression, and the desert of the post-World War II years, I have the pickings of the music of many great years. My favorites include both the rare and valuable and the more common and less valuable. Jimmie Rodgers' "The Southern Cannonball" is rare, for example, and in mint condition has commanded more than $100. His "T for Texas" is more easily found and costs perhaps a tenth of what you might pay for a copy of "Cannonball." I enjoy them equally.

The monetary value of old country music seems to follow a paradoxical rule. The more famous the artist was, the more likely it is that records will be around, and that they will be fairly inexpensive: larger quantities were made, and people saved them. Along with Jimmie Rodgers' "T for Texas," examples of the easy-to-find are Earl Johnson's "Hen Cackle" on OKeh, Gid Tanner's "Pass Around the Bottle" on Columbia and Charlie Poole's "Don't Let Your Deal Go Down," also on Columbia. There are, however, exceptions to this rule. The Carter Family was certainly famous, but their recording on Victor of "I Have an Aged Mother" is expensive. This is because the song was issued only on Montgomery Ward's label and was sold only through that firm's mail-order catalogue, contrary to the usual practice of issuing the same recording with several different labels for sale through a variety of retail channels.

Some records are valuable because of the label. Black Patti was in business for only half a year, and a record bearing that label may be worth hundreds of dollars. Victor's Timely Tunes label survived only three months of the Depression year of 1931 and its records, regardless of the performer, are so rare that some bring prices equal to those of Black Patti. At least two Timely Tunes performers are worth a special effort to locate—Gene Johnson and Jimmie Smith, both pseudonyms for a singer who became better known later as Gene Autry on labels that lasted longer than Timely Tunes.

All of these records were made before the introduction of the modern long-playing recording; they play only about three minutes per side, rotating at 78 revolutions per minute instead of 33⅓. A good way to find out about rare records and prices is to get on the mailing

Jimmie Rodgers, "The Singing Brakeman," was a national country-music star from the time he first recorded his yodeling style in 1927.

Because "hillbilly" was sometimes considered a demeaning characterization, Gennett tried the description of "Old Time Singin' & Playin' " for this 1927 label of songs by banjoist John Hammond.

Da Costa Woltz's Southern Broadcasters were not radio performers; Woltz (second from right) apparently hoped the name would help persuade Gennett to record them—and it did. The Broadcasters are shown here with 12-year-old Price Goodson, a recording-session vocalist.

A record made by the group above was produced by the Gennett record company for Herwin, a mail-order-house label. Few copies were made, so this title is now hard to find.

The rare Lonesome Ace label was used by William E. Meyer, a Virginia store owner. The name was meant to suggest Lindbergh, the Lone Eagle, and the motto apparently reflects a dislike of Jimmie Rodgers' yodel.

lists of people who sell old 78s by mail. There are a number of them, including Don Cleary of Fort Lauderdale, Florida; County Sales of Floyd, Virginia; and Record Research, of Brooklyn. You will find others in advertisements in periodicals listed at the end of this article. Some of these also print historical information—limited "discographies"—on performers and labels.

I do not treat my collection as a museum but as a music library. I use my records as they were meant to be used: I play them. Most modern hi-fi equipment can be set to play 78s; it is better to use present-day gear than an old phonograph, which reproduces sound badly and wears out the records quickly. The only danger lies in using the wrong stylus—you need an old-style fat needle to fit the 78 groove. This can be obtained from many sources that advertise in record-collectors' magazines.

If you find damaged records, it may not be necessary to pass them by. You can undo some of the harm. A record that is warped—because it has been stored flat instead of upright—can be straightened in an oven. Center the record on an empty soup can and heat it to 200°. When the record begins to soften, take it out, place it on a flat, level surface and weight it down—a stack of other records will do. If a chip has broken off and you have the chip, glue it back in place with fingernail polish; you will hear cracks, but the record will play.

But many old records survive in pristine condition. Once I followed a tip 25 miles down a corkscrew road in West Virginia to a hardware store in a grimy coal town. The store owner, a tiny, bald man, took me up to the balcony. There, perfectly stored upright and in mint condition, were more than 3,000 records—Brunswicks, Paramounts, old Victors, Vocalions (including three by famed banjoist Uncle Dave Macon). They had been there for almost 50 years. I picked out the ones I wanted, about 500 of them altogether, and brought them downstairs by the armfuls to where the old man was waiting. Now came the tricky part of the negotiation. As he began to clear his throat to speak, I said quickly, "How about a hundred for the lot?" He said, "Oh, all right." I whipped out five $20 bills, loaded the records into my car and sped back up the winding road.

For me, nothing beats the thrill of making finds like that one. And I know they are out there. There are still hundreds if not thousands of great old country-music recordings in lofts, attics and closets all over the United States, but particularly in the South. I know exactly where some of them are—I have already knocked at the back door and been told "Not today."

For related material, see the article on Jazz Memorabilia *in a separate volume of this encyclopedia.*

In 1928 and 1929 Edison produced "diamond disc" records, which could be played only on Edison equipment. Few were sold, and Edison supposedly destroyed thousands. As oddities, they are of moderate value.

The Lonely Eagles were cotton-mill workers, their selection a 19th Century minstrel song recorded by a Wisconsin chair-manufacturing company—in the '20s records were sold in furniture stores.

COUNTRY MUSIC / 37

Banjoist J. P. Nester's "Train on the Island"—his only recording—is shown in a sleeve promoting Victor artists. At top right is Jimmie Rodgers, at left center the Carter Family. Lesser luminaries are Bud Billings (top left), the Stamps Quartet with its accompanist (top center), the Georgia Yellowhammers (right center), and in the bottom row, J. W. Day, Tal Henry's North Carolinians, and Walter Kolomoku's Honolulans (right).

A Carter Family songbook cover suggests that the group composed the four songs listed; actually, they wrote only "My Clinch Mountain Home."

COUNTRY MUSIC / 39

This record was sold only briefly, and only through the Montgomery Ward catalogue. Many other Carter Family records, though more popular, were produced in greater quantity and are therefore less valuable.

Timely Tunes, made by Victor for Montgomery Ward, were offered at 24 cents each during the Depression. The low price attracted few buyers, few records were produced, fewer survive and those that do are valuable.

The "Colman & Harper" credited on this label were black artists Joe Evans and Arthur McClain, presumably renamed so that the records could be listed in the Perfect catalogue of songs by white artists.

Crown issued but 500 titles during the early 1930s, and cowboy singer Edward L. Crain's "Poor Boy" was one of the few of Crown's country music offerings, making it a collector's prize today.

40 / COUNTRY MUSIC

A recording by the Mississippi 'Possum Hunters for Victor cost about a quarter in 1932, but has since brought $100. As with most Depression records, very few copies were made.

Days after the infamous pair of bank robbers was shot in 1934, "Clyde Barrow and Bonnie Parker" was recorded by Bluebird. Copies can still be found, but one in good condition is a desirable collectible.

The Prairie Ramblers, a white group, recorded "Jug Rag" for the Conqueror label, sold by Sears, Roebuck and Co. Since most jug bands were made up of blacks, this recording is sought after.

COUNTRY MUSIC / 41

A Gene Autry songbook, put together by the movie cowboy and his collaborator, Jimmie Long, was published during the early years of the singer's career.

This 1929 record of Gene Autry doing a yodeling song is valuable only in mint condition. The song was so popular that most of the copies were played over and over until they wore out.

The Sons of the Pioneers were a group organized by singing cowboy star Roy Rogers, who had left it before this picture was taken. The group was known for its smooth harmony.

The first female country singer to sell more than one million records was Patsy Montana, whose songbook remained popular for 20 years after it came out in 1941.

42 / COUNTRY MUSIC

Charlie Poole, a banjoist from Haw River, North Carolina, was a forerunner of bluegrass musicians. He played with thumb and two fingers in the "rolling" style that allows individual notes to be heard separately.

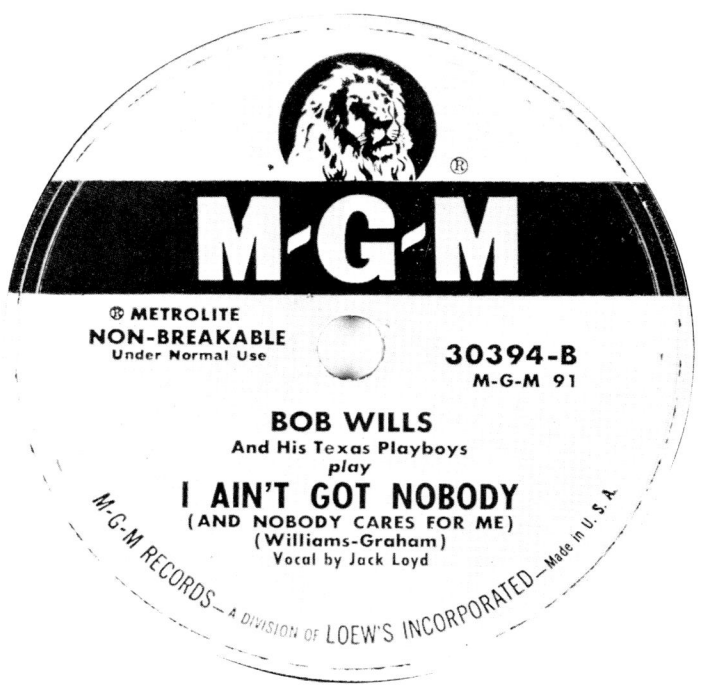

Bob Wills made "I Ain't Got Nobody" in 1935 for Vocalion, and it proved so popular that M-G-M issued a new release (above) in 1949. The M-G-M version is collectible, the earlier Vocalion a treasure.

A 1950 photograph shows mandolin player Bill Monroe with his Bluegrass Boys, for whom that style of country music is named. From the left are Vassar Clements, Joel Price, Jimmy Martin, Monroe, and Rudy Lyle. Two of their best-known songs are "Blue Moon of Kentucky" and "Rawhide." They recorded for Bluebird, Columbia and Decca.

COUNTRY MUSIC / 43

Sterling records were issued in small quantities, so Hank Williams' "Honky Tonkin'," made in 1947, is rare. At right is a Hank Williams songbook; the first edition, issued in 1949, is the most valuable.

This picture of Alton Delmore (left) and his brother, Rabon, who wrote more than 1,200 songs over two decades, was made around 1945, when the brothers starred in a radio show on WMC in Memphis.

MUSEUM AND LIBRARIES
Country Music Foundation Library and Media Center
Nashville, Tennessee 37203

John Edwards Memorial Foundation Library
University of California
Los Angeles, California 90024

PERIODICALS
Country Music, KBO Publishers, Inc., New York, New York 10016

John Edwards Memorial Foundation Quarterly, Folklore Center, UCLA, Los Angeles, California 90024

Goldmine, Arena Magazine, Fraser, Michigan 48026

BOOKS
Malone, Bill C., *Country Music U.S.A.* The University of Texas Press, 1974.

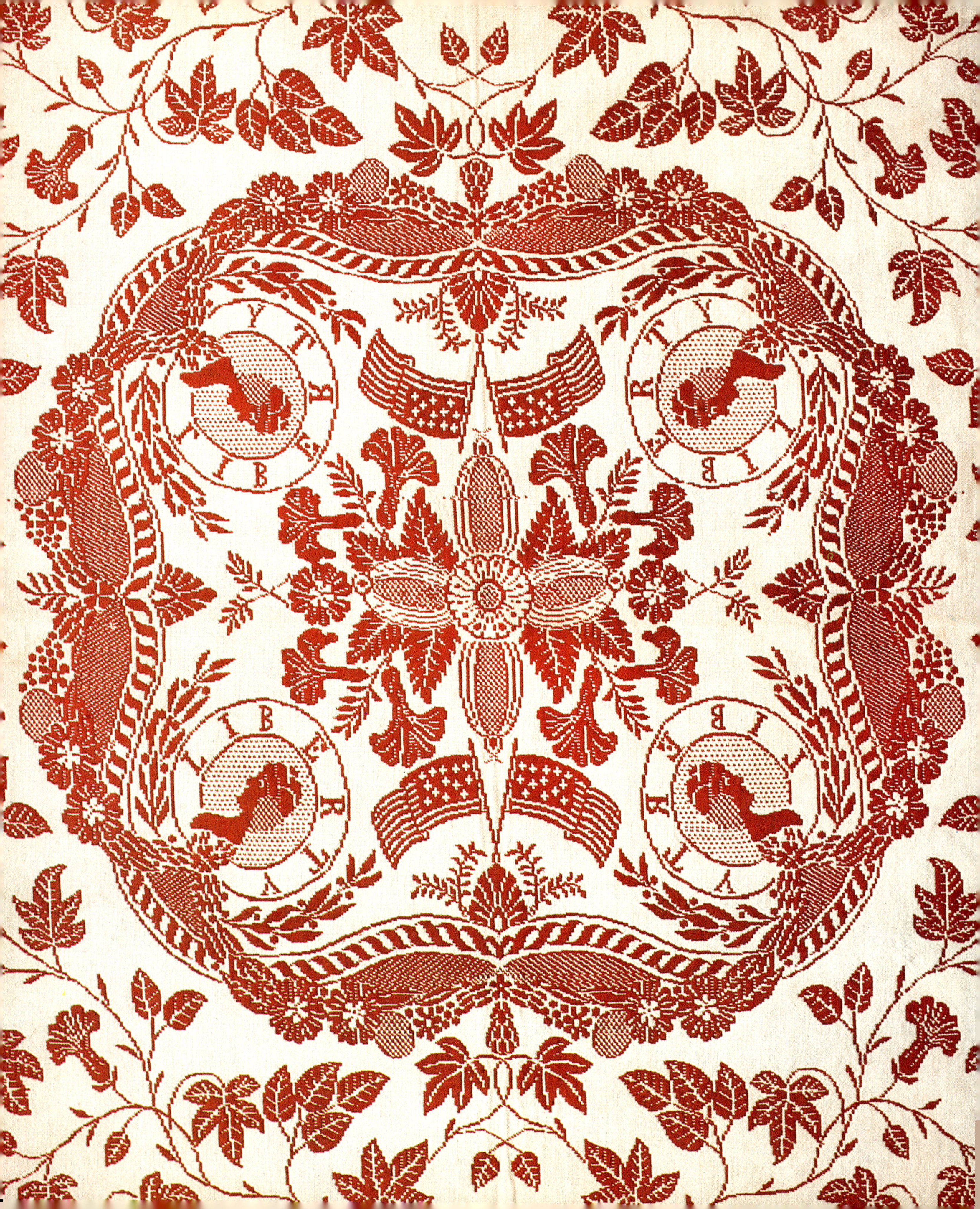
LIBERTY
LIBERTY
LIBERTY
LIBERTY

Coverlets
Bedding in Bygone Styles

In the early 1820s a New York weaver, James Alexander, began to run advertisements that intrigue modern collectors of coverlets, the brightly patterned spreads that were used to decorate beds in the 18th and 19th centuries. Alexander made two remarkable claims. He said that he was able for the first time to make coverlets with floral patterns, and, in addition, he reported that he had engaged a new assistant, recently arrived in America, who was familiar with the latest weaving developments in Europe.

Could Alexander have been hinting that he had obtained a Jacquard device—an automatic control using

Fred and Margaret Brusher, whose collection of coverlets includes some 200 early-American examples, look especially for the pictorial patterns of the Jacquard type.

printed cards to determine the patterns of cloth woven on a hand loom *(pages 48-49)*—and that he had in his shop a weaver who knew how to operate it? Most experts believe that the first Jacquard did not reach this country until several years after Alexander's advertisements appeared. However, it is known that the device had been perfected in France by 1805, and that by 1812 some 11,000 Jacquards were being used in Europe, not only as attachments for hand looms but with steam-powered weaving machines as well. I believe it is likely that Alexander was able to get hold of a Jacquard earlier than has been supposed. An 1821 coverlet that he produced *(page 51)* is certainly pictorial enough to suggest that it was the product of a Jacquard.

When the Jacquard reached the United States is a question of importance to collectors of coverlets. These bed coverings fall into two main categories so far as collectibility is concerned: geometric-patterned coverlets, woven on a variety of looms that were entirely hand-operated, and coverlets, most of them pictorial, made on hand looms fitted with the Jacquard attachment. The Jacquards are worth more than the others because the patterns are more interesting. In a 1978 auction cata-

The flags, Liberty heads and floral decorations on this 1850 coverlet, made by James Van Ness of Palmyra, New York, were achieved by adding the automatic control called a Jacquard to a hand loom.

A rare geometric coverlet was made entirely by hand in 1810 for Susan Beers, whose name was woven into it. The double-weave, two-layer design is reversible—blue on white and white on blue.

The overall pattern of this double-weave geometric coverlet, entirely hand-woven in two layers, is similar to one known as Virginia Beauty. *It contains a pine-tree border and repeated abstract designs that are variations of the "snowball," a common motif in geometric coverlets.*

logue the value of a Jacquard coverlet was estimated at $500 to $700, while the value of a geometric coverlet was estimated at $50 to $75.

Although there is disagreement on the date of the arrival of the Jacquard in the U.S., there can be little doubt that it was used on hand looms only briefly. Jacquard weavers soon began to feel competition from factory-made bedding. By the end of the Civil War the hand-woven coverlet—Jacquard or geometric—was practically gone from the marketplace. That ended an era that began in colonial days, when women wove geometric coverlets on hand looms at home and more affluent households patronized professional weavers.

The thrifty habit of using something until it falls to pieces has done away with many of the 18th Century linen-and-wool ("linsey-woolsey") coverlets. Still, some of these geometrics turn up now and then. A coverlet too tattered for display on the bed would be given a second career as a horse blanket. Farmers have used old coverlets to protect produce on the way to market. Many years ago one Southern collector who lived by a highway hired a helper to watch for passing tobacco trucks. When the watcher spotted a truck with a coverlet over its load he flagged down the truck and summoned the collector to dicker with the astonished driver.

A coverlet that might have ended up on a tobacco

Like the coverlet at left, this example of hand-woven geometric double weave has a border of pine trees, but they and the snowballs are stylized in a different way. Many regional variations of geometric motifs were made, and usually were given different names.

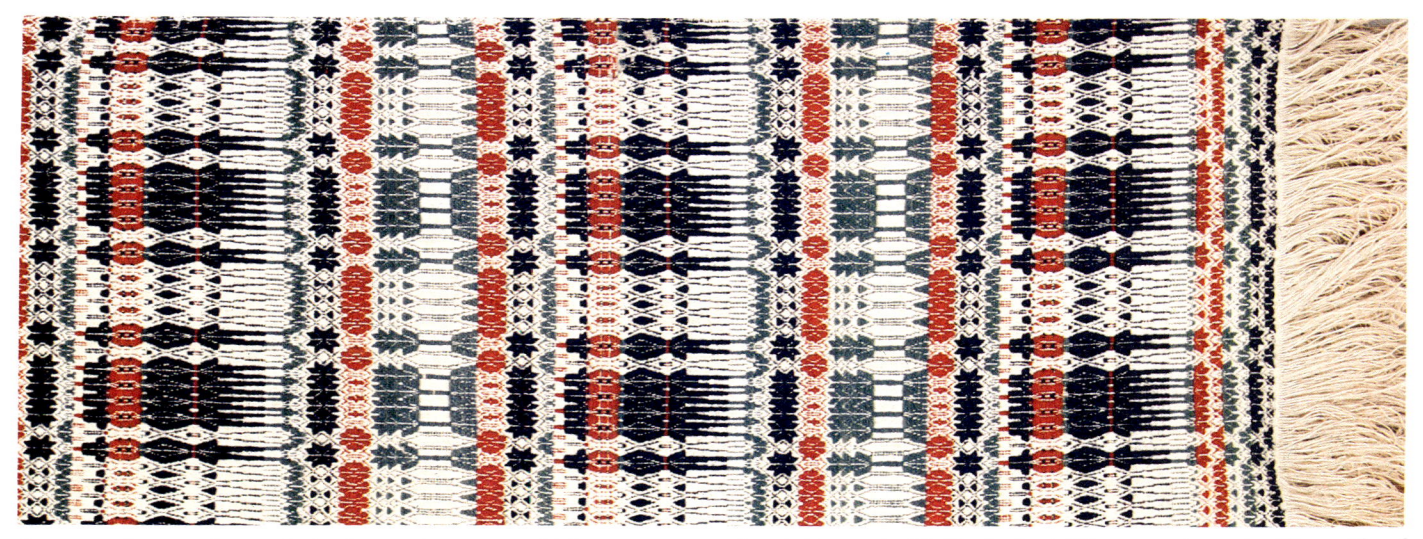

An unusual geometric coverlet in the overshot weave, which crosses one crosswise thread over several lengthwise ones, has stylized figures (reproduced sideways in this illustration). They may represent soldiers with red belts, blue hats and jackets, and light-blue shoes.

truck was likely to have been a geometric, a bold design made up of a single color contrasting with white or natural. In most such coverlets the color is in the wool yarn because the linen (and somewhat later, cotton) was difficult to dye and was left natural. With the introduction of the Jacquard, more complex designs led to greater use of color, and two or three colors became common in the Jacquard coverlets of the 1840s and 1850s.

Both geometric and Jacquard coverlets are classified according to weave. There are three principal weaves—overshot, single-weave and double-weave. Overshot is the simplest, the one most often used by home weavers. Its pattern is repeated throughout: the weft (crosswise) thread was made to skip three or more warp (lengthwise) threads at a time and to "float"—that is, to remain loose. The threads were skipped over in the same place for a number of rows, thus forming a square.

Single-weave coverlets can be distinguished by ribbing that runs the length of the fabric. The ribbing is made by weaving small groups of warp threads close together. A "tie-down" thread appears at regular intervals to interlock with the weft.

For the double-weave pattern two warps and two wefts were used, producing two layers of cloth. Double-weave patterns have sharper contrasts than overshot and single-weave patterns but, because they were difficult to produce, professional weavers made them only on special order.

Tracing the work of a particular professional weaver is difficult, since many weavers produced similar patterns and few order books or other records have been found. However, in a few cases the search is simplified by the fact that some Jacquard weavers dated and signed their work. The corners of a Jacquard may also show the name of the town or county where the weaver's shop was located, and this may be an important factor in determining the price of a coverlet as a collectible.

Many collectors pay well for coverlets woven near their homes. A Pennsylvania collector might offer $500 for a coverlet woven in Lancaster, while a collector in Ohio would think it worth $300. Not every collector can buy a Jacquard made in his own state because these devices are known to have been used only in New York, New Jersey, Pennsylvania, Maryland, Ohio, Iowa, Indiana, Illinois and Michigan; some Jacquards also were woven in Canada. Why the Jacquard was not used elsewhere is a question that puzzles historians of textiles.

Since the makers—and even the origin—of most coverlets are seldom known, value depends to a great extent on pattern. One coverlet whose pattern makes it very valuable is the Hempfield Railroad coverlet *(page 57)*—one of several apparently made to honor the opening of a line from Wheeling, West Virginia, to Washington, Pennsylvania. A coverlet with a similar border, though not one of the prized commemoratives, was auctioned early in 1978 for $5,500—a spectacular price.

Much coverlet buying and selling is done by auction and mail. Customarily, color photographs are sent to a prospective buyer to let him judge the look of a coverlet he is interested in. Be wary. Red and gold, two colors prized in coverlets, are difficult to judge from photographs. And catalogues prepared for auctions offer only black-and-white photographs as a rule. Before you buy a coverlet, look for fading color, tears, moth damage, soil and wear. To find worn spots hold the coverlet up to light and look for places where it shows through.

If there is any possibility that you might be offered a factory-made coverlet as hand-woven, extra caution is naturally called for. In the case of factory products of high quality, differentiation is difficult, even for an expert. Factory coverlets generally are more loosely woven and flimsier, being made mostly of cotton and wool that was lighter in weight than that used by hand weavers.

Like all old textiles, coverlets demand care in storing and cleaning. But, of course, the best place for a coverlet at home, if exposure to direct sunlight can be avoided, is the place for which it was made in the first place—a bed.

For related material, see the articles on Embroidery and Quilts in separate volumes of this encyclopedia.

The Punch-Card Loom

One of the landmarks of technology is the device for which Joseph Marie Jacquard of Lyons, France, obtained a French patent in 1805. The first complex automatic control, it used punch cards like those in modern business machines to determine the design woven by a loom, hand- or power-operated. It vastly expanded the versatility of the loom, simplifying the production of pictorial and curvilinear patterns as well as the traditional angular, geometric ones of manually controlled looms. As a result, coverlets made on Jacquard-controlled hand looms became the most wanted coverlets in the second quarter of the 19th Century, and today are the ones that most collectors seek.

The use of a Jacquard attachment does not alter the basic mode of weaving on a hand loom, by which warp and weft threads are interlaced. The warp threads are those that run the length of the fabric. The weft runs across the width of the fabric. The weft thread is wound on bobbins that are carried in the "shuttle," or "fly shuttle" (not visible in the drawing), which is moved back and forth to weave the weft thread over and under warp threads. What determines the pattern is the number and location of warp threads that one weft thread passes over, and the number and location of those it passes under.

Without a Jacquard, the weaver had to maneuver warp threads by hand, a process so slow and prone to error it limited the kinds of patterns that were practical. The Jacquard did the maneuvering in automated fashion. Its key element is a series of paper cards or metal plates perforated to make their holes match certain perforations in a rectangular "cylinder" that the cards pass over, the number and location of card holes depending on which step each card controls in forming the pattern. As a card is moved into position against the cylinder, needles activated by springs press up against it. Wherever a needle encounters a hole in the card, it passes through, and then through the matching hole in the cylinder. The needles that pass through activate heddles—cords attached to warp threads—lifting them. Needles stopped by the card cannot activate heddles, leaving their warp threads in place.

After the Jacquard sets the heddles to select the desired warp threads, the weaver sends the shuttle bearing a weft thread across the loom, under the lifted warp threads and over those remaining in place. Using the "beater," he then tucks the weft thread in place and pushes his foot treadle, turning the cylinder and pulling the next card into position for the next weft thread. As many as several thousand punch cards were required for a single coverlet.

COVERLETS / 49

In this 19th Century drawing, a Jacquard loom makes a narrow strip of cloth, not a coverlet, but the technique is the same. The pattern, coded on punch cards, is read by a cylinder and needles to lift certain heddle cords tied to warp threads. The weaver uses the fly-shuttle control to send shuttle and weft thread across the loom. Woven cloth rolls onto the cloth beam.

The eagle woven by a Jacquard automatic control into the corner of an 1847 coverlet identifies it as the design of Elman Tyler. The customer's name appears below the eagle. This coverlet is special because it is all wool (not the usual cotton and wool) and is done in Christmasy colors.

COVERLETS / 51

The coverlet at left was made for Susan Wilkin, whose name appears in the corner, by James Alexander of New York in 1821. The pictorial pattern suggests that it was woven with a Jacquard attachment—although the device is generally believed not to have been in use in America before 1824. The pillars and the crossed compass and square above them in the border are emblems of the society of Masons, to which Alexander belonged.

Mary S. Palmer took her coverlet (left) with her when she moved to Michigan in the 1840s from New York. The lion in the corner was the symbol used by Jacquard weaver Harry Tyler of Jefferson County, New York, whose son Elman designed the coverlet on the opposite page. Elman considered his father's lion too British and replaced it with an eagle.

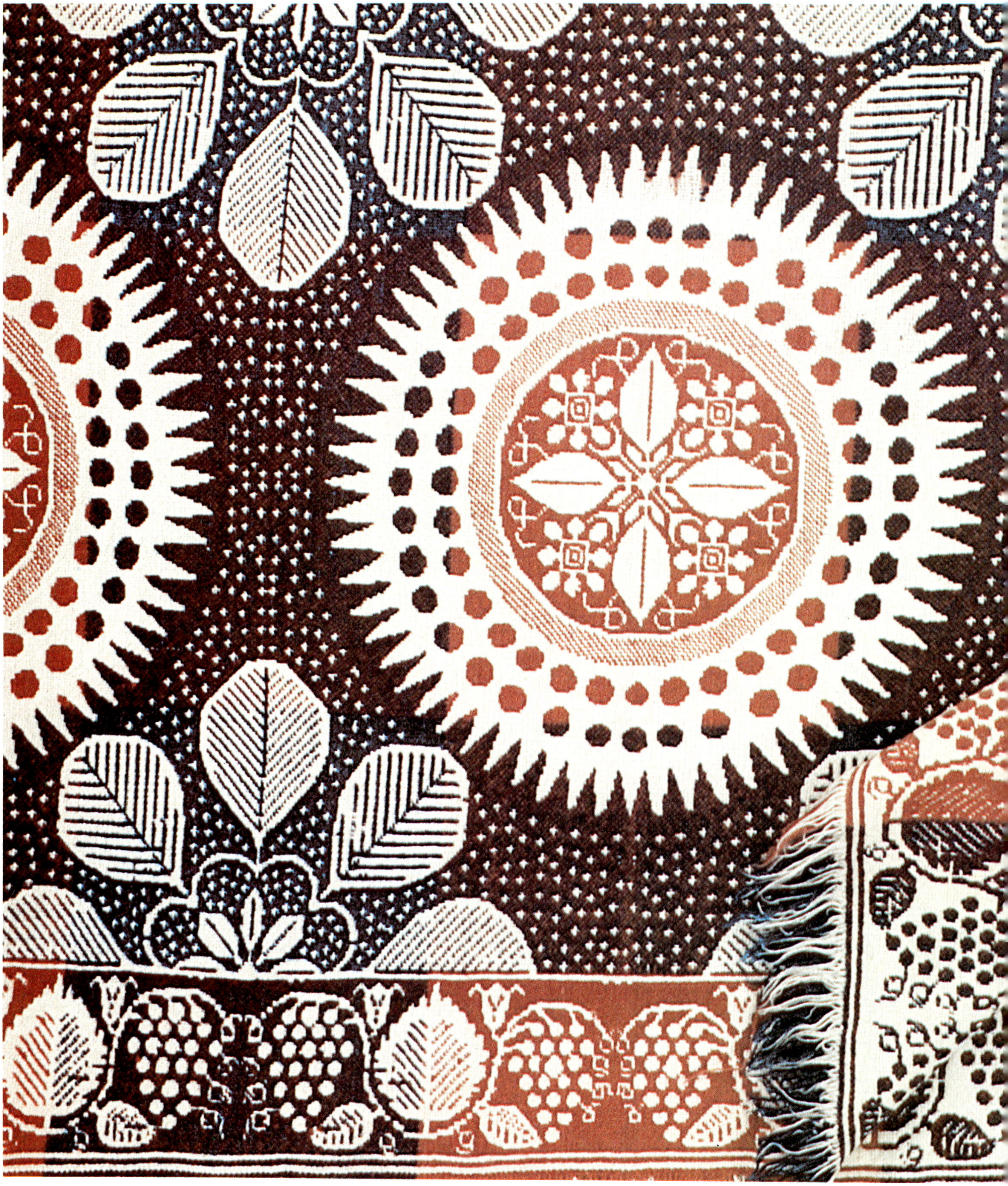

This red, blue and cream-colored Jacquard coverlet was woven in the 1850s by the weaver whose name and location appear in the corner. The buildings seen in the border may represent those in the town of Gallipolis.

This 1850 Jacquard coverlet is exceptional because of its material, wool rather than the usual mixture of wool and cotton; because of its colors, a rare combination of rust and brown; but mainly because of its maker: Sarah La Tourette of Fountain County, Indiana, the only woman known to have been a professional Jacquard weaver. She learned the craft from her father, and after he died she carried on the business with her brother Henry. The collector obtained the coverlet from descendants of the Isaac Foster family, for whom Sarah La Tourette made it.

This red and blue Jacquard coverlet with rose and eagle motifs was made in Pennsylvania in 1843 in the single weave. The coverlet was woven in two strips and then seamed up the center to make it the desired size.

The main flower-and-lyre pattern of a double-weave coverlet of the 1850s is not uncommon, but the border is: it depicts the balcony of a bawdy house from which women can be seen waving. The coverlet was made for Lillian Stuckey, a Western madam who was known as Diamond Tooth Lil.

56 / COVERLETS

Abram William Van Doren of Michigan wove the coverlet above for Charles Kimball in 1848. The main motif is medallions with lilies; the border is decorated with small birds.

The distinctive border design of the Jacquard coverlet at right is called, for reasons unknown, Penelope's Flower Pot. The weaver took care to make his own identity clear.

A Jacquard of the 1850s is one of several coverlets, now very rare, made to celebrate the beginning of service on the Hempfield Railroad (misspelled on the coverlet). The portrait woven into the corner is of Thomas M. T. McKennan, the first president of the line.

58 / COVERLETS

The downcast faces visible in the corners of this coverlet mystify collectors. The main designs—called medallions and tiles and closely resembling quilt patterns—are strikingly geometric, although the coverlet was woven on a Jacquard loom, normally used for pictorial designs.

A red and white Jacquard was woven in Canada in 1901 by William and John Noll of Petersburg, Ontario, who first set up shop there around 1868. John Noll's son, also named John, continued the family weaving business until 1930.

MUSEUMS

The Art Institute of Chicago
Chicago, Illinois 60603

Farmers' Museum
Cooperstown, New York 13326

Greenfield Village and Henry Ford Museum
Dearborn, Michigan 48121

Merrimack Valley Textile Museum
North Andover, Massachusetts 01845

The Newark Museum
Newark, New Jersey 07101

Pennsylvania Farm Museum of Landis Valley
Lancaster, Pennsylvania 17601

Shelburne Museum
Shelburne, Vermont 05482

COLLECTORS ORGANIZATIONS
Colonial Coverlet Guild of America
7931 Birchdale Avenue
Elmwood Park, Illinois 60635

BOOKS
Burnham, Harold and Dorothy, *Keep Me Warm One Night.* University of Toronto Press, 1972.

Davison, Mildred, and Christa C. Mayer-Thurman, *Coverlets.* The Art Institute of Chicago, 1973.

Heisey, John W., Gail C. Andrews and Donald R. Walters, *A Checklist of American Coverlet Weavers.* Colonial Williamsburg Foundation, 1978.

Laury, Jean Ray, *Quilts and Coverlets.* Van Nostrand Reinhold Co., 1970.

Montgomery, Pauline, *Indiana Coverlet Weavers and their Coverlets.* Hoosier Heritage Press, 1974.

Safford, Carleton L., and Robert Bishop, *America's Quilts and Coverlets.* E. P. Dutton and Co., 1972.

Cowboy Gear
Workaday Relics of the Old West

When I started my career as an artist painting illustrations for Western magazines in the 1950s, the American cowboy had long been portrayed working with gear he had never used. Hollywood was the worst offender—movies gave cowboys a shallow, low-slung open holster strapped to the thigh. That kind of holster was developed around 1910 so Wild West show performers and movie cowboys could show off their skill as quick-draw artists. It could never have held a cowboy's pistol securely while he was riding, roping or branding. Cowboy holsters were narrow and deep, and designed to be worn at the waist.

I knew of this kind of misrepresentation and, determined to be historically accurate, I set out to collect real

Joe Grandee, the first Official Artist of Texas, is noted for his paintings of Western subjects. He began collecting cowboy gear in the 1950s.

cowboy gear and costumes as models in my painting. I spent my first collecting dollars on research—buying books and traveling to museums to study authentic photographs and prints of the period, and the paintings of such 19th Century artists as Frederic Remington and C. M. Russell, who went West and painted from life. In their paintings you can see honest depiction of the gear actually used by cowboys in their work—saddles, guns, spurs, lariats, chaps and the clothing they wore on and off the range. Soon I was collecting as many of these things as I could find.

I have since discovered that there are other sources that can help verify the authenticity of things that turn up in antique shops and secondhand stores. Catalogues can be ordered from auction houses specializing in Old West material; their names and addresses appear in advertisements found in *Shotgun News (box, page 71)*. These will give auction prices that serve as guidelines. The catalogues put out by 19th Century saddle makers—which are themselves collectible—picture and describe saddles and virtually everything else in leather a working cowboy used. These catalogues can be bought at gun shows or through dealers in cowboy gear.

From information that I obtained in this way, I discovered that all American cowboy gear derives from two principal sources. To identify cowboy gear with any certainty, you need to know, first, which items come from which source and, second, how and when each came to be adapted to the cowboy's specific needs.

One category consists of gear originally developed by and for Mexican *vaqueros,* the continent's first cowboys, who worked all across the Southwest from Texas to California beginning in the early 1700s. The cowboy saddle was adapted from the Mexican type and so were chaps, cowboy hats, spurs and the roping lariat. The other category comprises military surplus brought West after the Civil War, when the Great Plains cattle boom was just getting under way. Guns, holsters, cartridge belts, canteens, boots and jackets—issued for field campaigns—were also useful in peacetime on the range. To a collector, the more interesting among such diverse items are naturally those directly involved in working with cattle—chaps, spurs, guns and holsters and, most important, saddles.

His saddle was a cowboy's most valued possession. For virtually all his waking hours he sat on it; when he slept out on the range it served as his pillow. It was a saddle developed for his requirements in riding, herding cattle and roping them for branding. The rawest tenderfoot could not mistake a modern saddle for one a cowboy could have used. The fronts, or "forks," of 19th Century saddles, called A-fork saddles, slope down sharply from the horn, and the seats are deep, with high "cantles" at their backs. Modern forks, by contrast, swell out into wide fronts and the backs are lower, and most modern saddles have padded seats.

Saddles are among the more plentiful cowboy items, but they vary greatly in value. One useful guideline is the maker's stamp. Some of the more famous are S. D. Myers of Sweetwater (later El Paso), Texas; E. L. Gallatin of Cheyenne; J. B. Sickles of St. Louis; R. T. Frazier of Pueblo, Colorado; and the Mile City Saddlery Company of Mile City, Montana. The makers' stamps may be on the back of the seat or on the fenders or side flaps; sometimes they are elsewhere and have to be looked for; other times you find only initials. A fine antique saddle

For his painting "Butch Cassidy at Hole in the Wall"—the settlement in Wyoming that the celebrated outlaw used as a hideout—the collector depicted clothing and equipment in his collection.

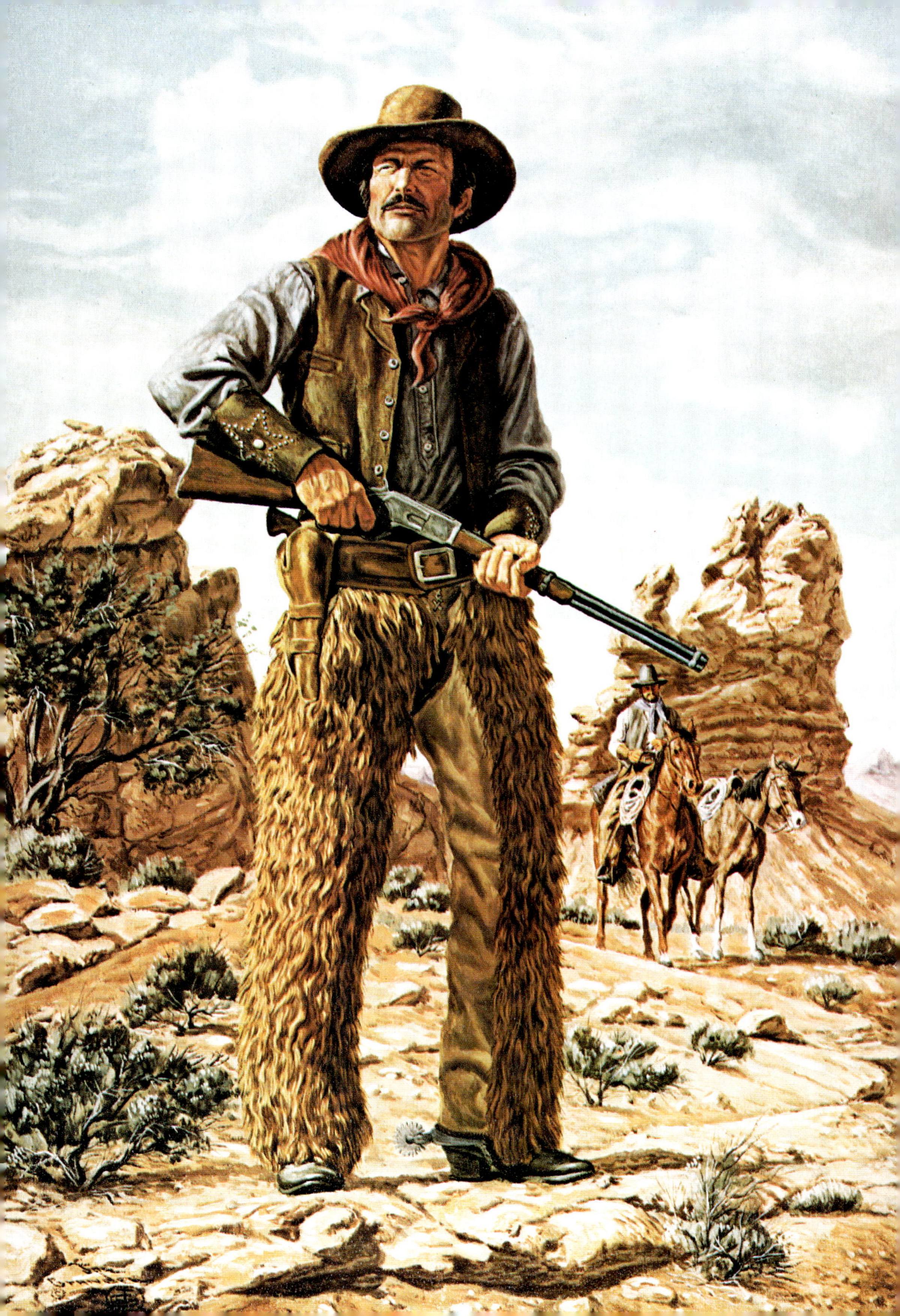

Mexican vaqueros, the original cowboys, used iron spurs with large-spiked rowels. This pair has jingle bobs, silver inlays in the heel bands, and long shanks with hooks that curl upward to guard the chaps.

An American set of spurs, with smaller rowels than the Mexican pair shown at top, was made around 1880 in California. The spurs are made of iron and have overlays of silver.

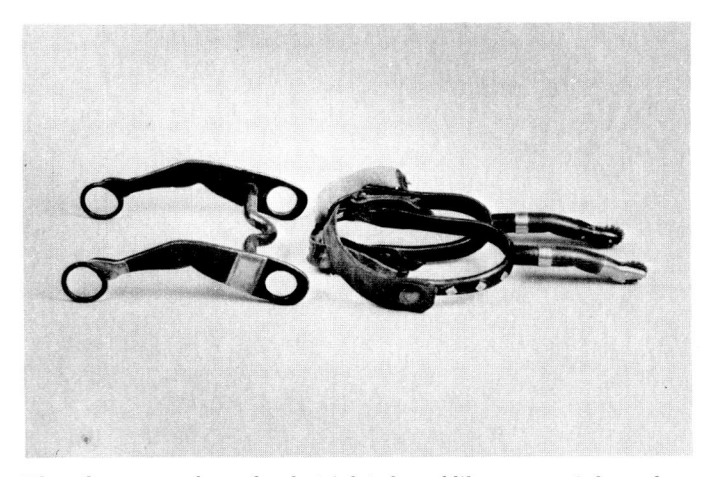

These fancy spurs have shanks (right) shaped like a woman's leg—from which they get their name, "gal-leg" spurs. This pair, shown with its matching bit (left), was made about 1910.

that has the maker's stamp can be worth anywhere from $100 to more than $1,000. Condition is important: a good purchase is a saddle that is well preserved, uncracked but polished from long wear.

Similar criteria apply to chaps. A maker's stamp may be pressed into the leather, and the saddle makers mentioned above are the names to look for. Material is a distinctive clue to age in the case of chaps. Period chaps are distinguishable from modern ones made for rodeos and Hollywood costumes by their thick, well-aged leather, close, meticulous stitching, and reinforced construction.

The third major item of leather—the pistol holster—is judged somewhat differently from chaps or saddles. Holsters are easier to date because those that were made prior to 1873 were designed to fit exactly the contours of specific guns. As a result the dates of pre-1873 holsters correspond to the dates of the guns for which they were made. After 1873 fewer gun models were made and many side arms could fit any holster. If you can identify the gun—pistol, rifle or carbine—for which a holster was made, you can date the holster. Unlike other items of cowboy equipment, guns are accurately documented in many books and catalogues available in libraries. These sources contain illustrations to help match gun to holster. In many cases they either depict or specify serial and patent numbers, which provide a way to establish the date of manufacture of the weapon. The same is true of long guns: rifles and carbines.

Many old cowboy pistols were military models, and so were the holsters. But while the guns were generally used unchanged, the holsters were not. With few exceptions, the military models had flaps to cover the gun butts. Although a cowboy was less likely to use his gun for quick-draw shoot-outs on Main Street than to kill snakes or wolves, or to turn a stampeding herd by firing into the air, he did need to have ready access to the weapon in an emergency. The time spent undoing a flap might be crucial. Some cowboys, therefore, began to cut off the flaps of military holsters.

Much of this old leather equipment was so sturdily made that many examples survive in good condition. Even less subject to the deterioration of age is one of the most distinctively attractive types of the cowboy's gear—his spurs. A poor cowboy newly arrived in the West would sometimes buy cheap Mexican spurs with large-spiked rowels—wheels at the back of the spur—but as soon as he could afford to, he would buy American spurs with smaller rowels. Mexican spurs are still being made by Mexican craftsmen in the style of three centuries ago and are distinguishable from old ones only by differences in wear and patina.

A 19th Century cowboy's dream—shared by collectors today—was to own a pair of silver-mounted dress spurs. To be perfect, the spurs had to bear the name of a

Cowboy boots of the 1870s, like those shown at left, were modeled after the Civil War types, which had low heels, narrow, flat toes and straight tops. At center is a later pair, probably made in the 1890s, with curved tops cut for decoration and 2-inch-high heels. The boots at right, which were made after the turn of the century, have "mule-ear" straps hanging over the tops to make them easier to pull on.

leading American maker—the last-name only, because that was all that spurmakers customarily used. Both Crockett and Kelly usually put their names inside the heel bands; the names of other makers, like Garcia, Bass, Boone, Bianchi and McChesner can be found almost anywhere on the spur.

Of all cowboy gear, the hardest to find in decent condition is clothing. Leather boots and beaver-felt hats have survived better than clothing made of denim, such as the famous Levis, or cotton or wool shirts, canvas jackets, coats and bandanas.

Boots can be identified and dated by style and shape, as shown in the photograph on page 63. Old hats, made first from wool, beaver fur or mink fur, and later from rabbit fur, also can be dated by style, but only loosely *(page 70)*. Precise dating of hats is practically impossible, even with experience. You can be sure a hat is valuable if you can identify its band as horsehair, because such a band can itself be worth up to $50. The only guideline is to be aware of collecting trends. When hats with the biggest brims and highest crowns are sought after by collectors, those become the valuable ones, soon to be superseded in desirability by some other style.

For a long time, living in the West was a distinct advantage for a collector of cowboy gear. Any roadside junk shop, pawn shop or old saddlery might have a valuable find. Many stores in the West were boarded up when boom-and-bust cycles came to bust, and merchandise was sometimes left in them when the stores were abandoned. In addition, a Mexican custom caused many stocks of equipment to be similarly interred. In border-town stores started by Mexican patriarchs, descendants sometimes closed the store as a monument to the old man when he died. This happened in Rio Grande City in Texas, where a store was closed, with its stock inside, for 50 years before the heirs liquidated it.

I benefited once from a similar situation in Iowa, far from traditional cow country, where an auctioneer's ad led me to a dry-goods store boarded up in the 1880s. Here I found a treasure-trove of cowboy gear, including a shirt with bow tie attached—a touch of dandified dressing not usually associated with the cowboy.

Such a find in areas that saw few, if any, real cowboys is not rare. Avid collecting and tourist buying have dried up most Western sources, and the hunting is now as good in the East as it is in the West. Joe Gish, a friend, fellow Texan and collector, recently got one of his finest pairs of angora chaps from a trunk in Pennsylvania. The chaps were made in Oregon and bought by a Pennsylvanian during a one-year sojourn in the West as a cowboy. His descendants had been preserving them against moth damage since 1919 and they are practically perfect. The chaps must have been a little too long for the original owner—the only wear that is apparent is on the very bottom.

For related material, see the articles on Civil War Equipment and Guns in separate volumes of this encyclopedia.

EARLY WESTERN SADDLE 1830-1840

COLORADO SADDLE, 1885-1890

MILITARY-TREE SADDLE, LATE 1860s

American cowboys began with Mexican saddles like the one at top left, made by applying wet rawhide to "trees"—wooden frameworks—then stitching it tight. As it dried, it shrank and was molded to the tree. At left is a saddle adapted from a U.S. Cavalry type, made on a cavalry tree. A wooden horn presumably was added, as most military saddles had no horn. The saddle at top right is in the style most common in the West after the 1880s. The steep cantle at the rear steadied the rider; the leather stirrup covers, or tapaderas, protected his feet.

TEXAS SADDLE, 1880

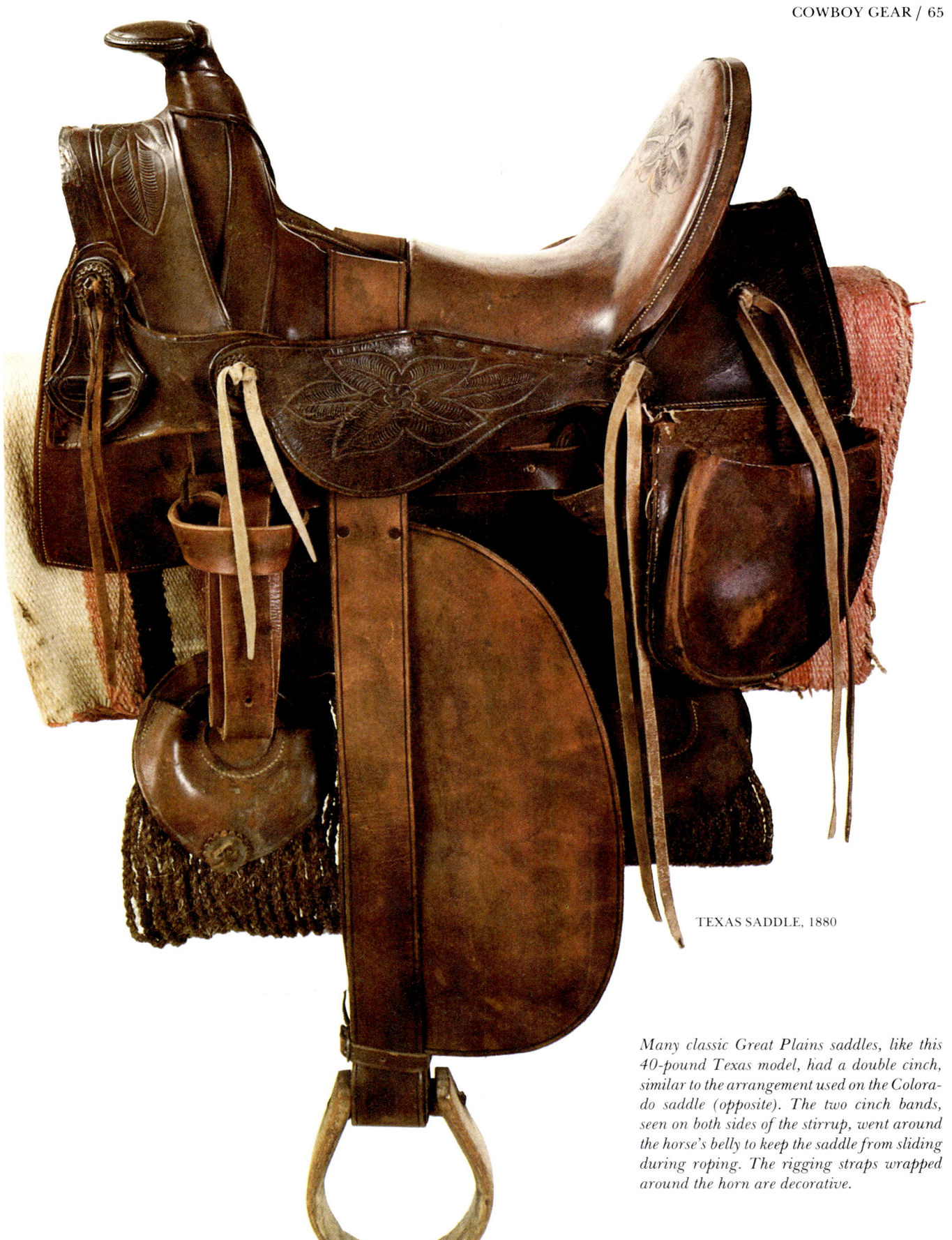

Many classic Great Plains saddles, like this 40-pound Texas model, had a double cinch, similar to the arrangement used on the Colorado saddle (opposite). The two cinch bands, seen on both sides of the stirrup, went around the horse's belly to keep the saddle from sliding during roping. The rigging straps wrapped around the horn are decorative.

66 / COWBOY GEAR

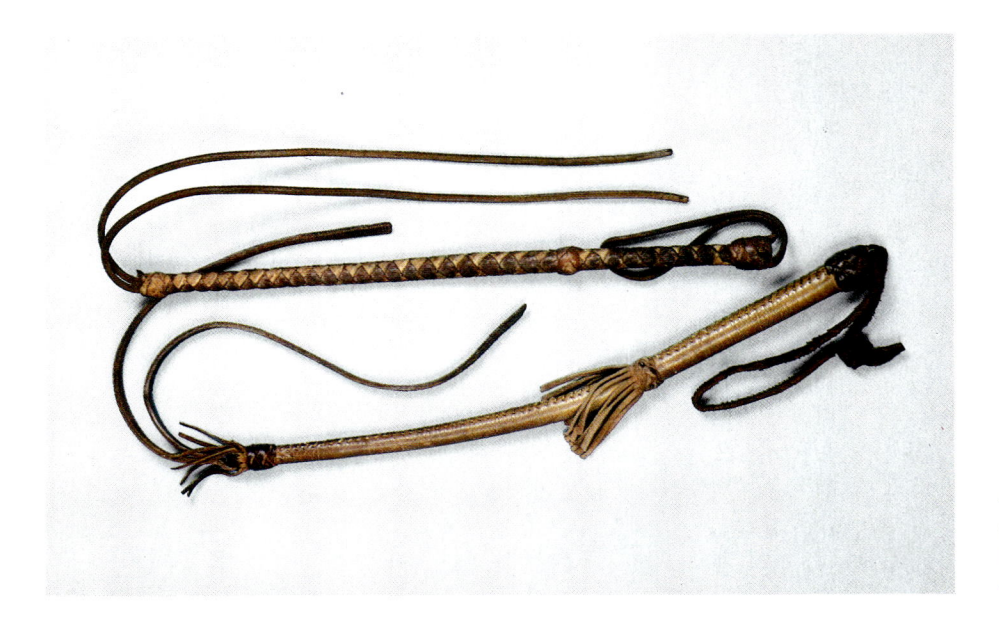

A cowboy would seldom mount up without a quirt, or short whip, like the ones shown here. Quirts were generally about 2 feet long, with a handle of braided rawhide.

Above are a bit and a leather headstall. Headstalls were also made of braided horsehair but these, being vulnerable to moths, are rare.

Range equipment included braided rawhide lariats and hobbles, one at the right of the lariat and one encircled by the lariat, which were used to shackle horses. Sometimes a horse was tethered to an iron picket pin like the one alongside the lariat.

COWBOY GEAR / 67

The evolution of the holster from military gear to cowboy gear is traced in the five examples above. Army surplus was at first used unchanged: 1846 open-topped (at bottom), then the 1850 flap-covered model. Later the flap was cut off (third from bottom). A wide belt loop was included in an early Western-made holster (fourth from bottom), leading by 1880 to the traditional type at top.

These two guns, the .44-caliber 1876 Winchester rifle (top) and 1873 carbine, were the models popular on the range; each is shown with its saddle scabbard. The rifle's longer barrel made it more accurate, but most cowboys preferred the carbine because it was lighter. During the late 1870s, many cowboys switched from the Colt .45 pistol to the Colt .44 because its ammunition was interchangeable with the Winchester's.

These cowboy shirts, part of an 1880s stock undisturbed until the 1960s, include one (far right) with attached bow tie—the only one of its kind known.

An English-style vest provided a cowboy with pockets for his tobacco, tally books for use in counting cattle, playing cards and perhaps family pictures. The one shown above is canvas and from the 1880s.

Hip-length woolen coats like this one were the usual winter attire on the Southern ranges, where the climate did not require heavier garments such as the fur shown on page 71.

COWBOY GEAR / 69

Buckskin gloves—these date from about 1870—were worn to avoid rope burns. The flared-cuff style (left) was based on the cavalry glove. Cowboys liked "fancied-up" gloves with fringes and beadwork (right).

Leather cuffs were worn on the wrists for protection from rope burns while branding. These cuffs are ornamented with basket-weave stamping and nickel spots, dating them to the 1880s.

These "shotgun" chaps—so called because of their shape—can be dated to around 1870 by the straight waistband. By about 1890, waistbands dropped to a V shape in front (right).

Angora "woollies" of 1890 were worn on the cold Northern ranges in wintertime. Angora chaps were the warmest, but others, of buffalo, bear or wolfhide, all with the fur left on, were also used.

70 / COWBOY GEAR

A plainsman's hat with a wide brim and a low, round crown was the kind worn by Mexican vaqueros in Texas, by early American fur trappers and by the first American cowboys.

Vaqueros on the West Coast preferred a flatter crown than their fellows in Texas (top). The crown of this beaver hat from California peaks slightly in the style that began to be popular in the 1830s.

Above is a Plains-style hat, dating from the 1870s or '80s. American cowboy hats then began to move to high crowns because they were found to be cooler than the low plainsman's crown.

The pinched crown of the "Montana peak" style came into popularity in that state in the 1890s. Its narrower brim helped the hat stay in place on the windy Northern ranges.

A cowboy hat of the period from 1900 to 1930, with a deep crease down the center, a big "10-gallon" crown and a wide brim, is the kind made famous by such early movie cowboys as Tom Mix.

At first, cowboys wore Mexican ponchos in the rain. From the 1880s on, long sailor's slickers like this, to cover saddle and rider, were ordered from Gloucester, Massachusetts. Black ones are rare; most were yellow.

Long, heavy winter coats were essential on the cold Northern ranges. This is bearskin with matching mittens. Also worn were cloth coats, some with fur linings, and military-issue buffalo coats.

MUSEUMS AND LIBRARIES
Buffalo Bill Historical Center
Cody, Wyoming 82414

Montana Historical Society Library
Helena, Montana 59601

National Cowboy Hall of Fame
Oklahoma City, Oklahoma 73111

Panhandle-Plains Historical Museum
Canyon, Texas 79016

Texas Ranger Hall of Fame
Waco, Texas 76703

PERIODICALS
The Antique Trader, Babka Publishing Co., Dubuque, Iowa 52001

Shotgun News, Snell Publishing Co. Inc., Hastings, Nebraska 68901

BOOKS
Beitz, Les, *Treasury of Frontier Relics: A Collector's Guide.* A. S. Barnes and Co., Inc., 1977.

Forbis, William H., *The Cowboys.* TIME-LIFE BOOKS, 1973.

McCracken, Harold, *The American Cowboy.* Doubleday & Company, Inc., 1973.

Tyler, Ron, *The Cowboy.* Ridge Press Book, William Morrow & Company, Inc., 1975.

Vernam, Glenn, *Man on Horseback.* Harper & Row, 1964.

Ward, F. E., *The Cowboy at Work.* Hastings House, 1958.

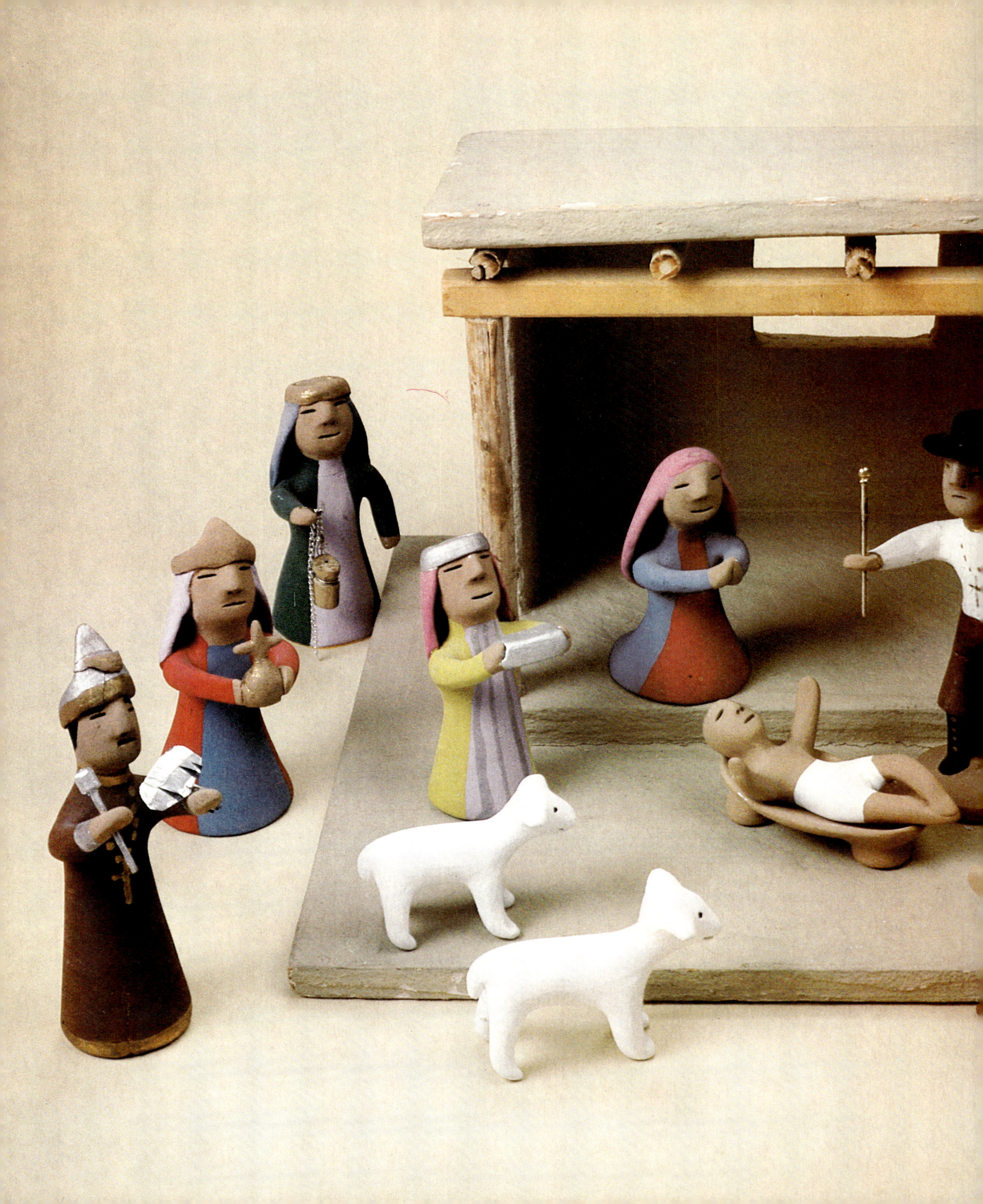

Crèches
Miniature Mangers

Crèches—three-dimensional models of the Nativity—have been part of the Christmas tradition for nearly 1,000 years. They center around a figure of the infant Jesus lying in a crib, generally with a small manger as a backdrop. In many the child is attended by small groups of figures—the Madonna and Joseph, the Three Kings bearing gifts, a few shepherds and their sheep. The figures may be freestanding, glued in place, or carved in low relief on a background. More elaborate versions may include a cow and a donkey, angels, cherubs, camels, elephants, slaves or villag-

At an elaborate Christmas Eve ceremony each year, Earl Kage and his friends unpack and set up his 72 crèches from all parts of the world.

ers. The figures may range in height from half an inch to a foot or more.

The height of the crèche-builder's art was reached in 18th Century Naples, where puppet-like figures with beautiful terra-cotta or wood heads were created. They stood as high as 18 inches and were elaborately dressed.

Peddlers and other travelers eventually carried the crèches throughout Europe, and now the crèche is an international symbol of Christmas. Craftsmen in the Provence region of France to this day produce the traditional small earthenware figures known as *santons* ("little saints," in the provincial dialect) that their ancestors began making early in the 19th Century. Cast in molds (many of which have been passed down for several generations) and painted by hand, the figures represent people of the area dressed in the costumes of the early 19th Century. Old *santons,* whose colors and lines have been softened over the years, are the ones that collectors prize the most.

Because crèches are unpacked and handled every Christmas, it is difficult to find older folk-art crèches that are still intact. Examples of the art from the 19th Century and earlier are particularly scarce and expensive. The work of the best Neapolitan artisans, for in-

The figures of a modern crèche created by a Pueblo Indian craftsman are of fired and painted clay; the stable is adobe. Although the Kings and shepherds are dressed in traditional-looking robes, Joseph wears a wide, flat-brimmed hat and high boots that suggest Spanish style.

Made of plaster in Prussia more than a century ago, this crèche has no freestanding figures. It follows the bas-relief style of early altar pieces, from which crèches evolved.

This unpainted devotional scene, about 7 inches high, was carved in Germany in the 20th Century. The figures represent two angels and the infant Jesus lying in his crib, bathed in the light of Bethlehem's star.

stance, rank as museum pieces; in 1978 a dealer in Naples offered a section of a crèche that was made for a church for about $3,000.

My own collection, assembled over 17 years, includes 72 crèches. A few are old, but most are recent examples reflecting the ways different people have depicted a 2,000-year-old story. Some are carved wood (painted or left plain), some are plaster, others are papier-mâché, cardboard, bamboo, molded plastic and clay. They come from all over the world and suggest the wide variety of cultures dominated, influenced or somehow touched by Christianity: Southwestern American Indian, Japanese, Nigerian, Swedish, Italian, Mexican, Colombian, Peruvian, Portuguese and Chinese. I even have an Israeli crèche made for American tourists.

Recently made, reasonably priced crèches are found —especially during the Christmas season—at craft fairs, Christmas shops, department stores, gift shops and antique shops. When Nativity sets are out of season, many stores keep them stored away, so even if you do not see a crèche on display, ask the shopkeeper about any that might be in a back room.

Garage sales and auctions are also good places to look for complete crèches and even individual pieces that may have been owned by the same family for generations. Look especially for doll auctions, at which crèches may be incorrectly identified as dollhouses and dolls.

Prices you may expect to hear bid are $250 for a fine Neapolitan figure, less than half that for a 19th Century wooden Mexican figure. And for about half of the Mexican price you might find the small papier-mâché figures that not long ago were available in dime stores in the United States.

Since I like to collect examples of as many international styles as possible, I ask friends who are traveling abroad to keep an eye out for crèches in museum shops and government-run tourist shops, where examples of local crafts are likely to be sold. Crèches are sold each year at the Christmas markets held in most European cities, such as Madrid, Marseilles and Nuremberg. It helps to know the local name for crèches. The word Americans use is actually the French name. In England it is a crib, in Germany *krippe,* in Italy *presepio,* in Spain *nacimiento,* in Portugal *belém,* in Latin America *santos.*

Generally, I do not pass up any unusual style of crèche, even if I find it in a dime store. A particular crèche may be produced in great quantity one year and never made again, eventually becoming a valuable collectible. A plastic crèche made in Hong Kong in the mid-1950s sold in this country for 87 cents; I would not part with mine for less than $50.

For related material, see the article on Christmas Tree Ornaments in a separate volume of this encyclopedia.

Spanish angels of the 18th Century, more than 2 feet tall, were probably created for a wealthy family's crèche. Like many in southern Europe, they are wood covered with gesso and painted. The collector paid about $250 for these in 1960. In less than 20 years their value quadrupled.

76 / CRÈCHES

Above is an overall view of a crèche from Peru, with details at the right. It is nearly 5 feet high and deep. The creator, Peruvian painter Hilario Mendovil, placed the Holy Family before a platform bearing a heavenly orchestra. Near the top are another Madonna and Babe (upper detail). The satanic scenes (right) appear on the sides of the platform steps.

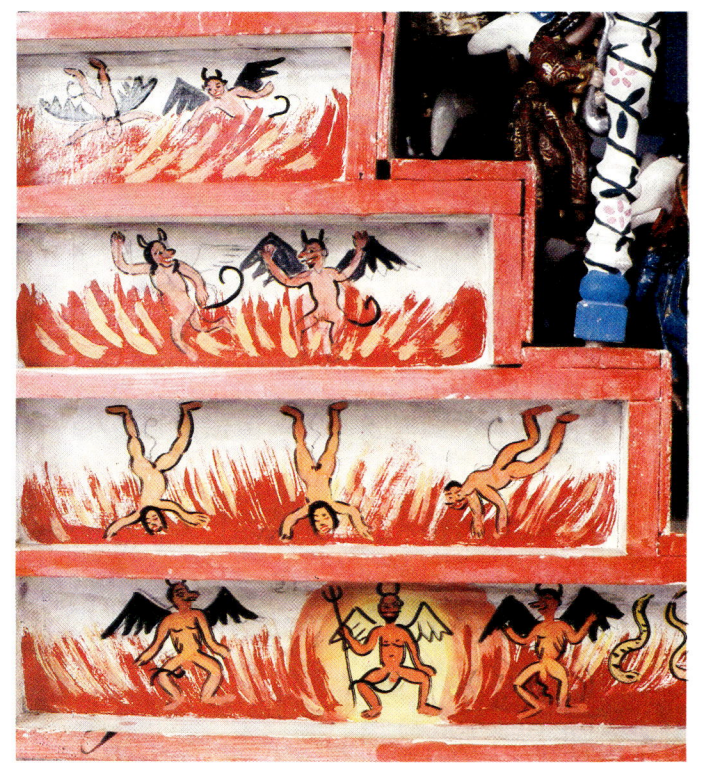

CRÈCHES / 77

An owl, a deer, a cat, a fox and an array of other forest and farmyard animals join the traditional ox, donkey and camels in a contemporary crèche from Germany. Showing animals not mentioned in the Nativity story is a recent innovation.

A pre-World War II export to the United States from Germany, this painted plaster crèche was probably sold in dime stores. Although made in quantity, it was flimsy and easily damaged; this one is a rare survivor.

A villager in Colombia, South America, modeled ceramic crèche figures, using local costumes for some, traditional robes for the Three Kings. Each of the figures is about 10 inches high.

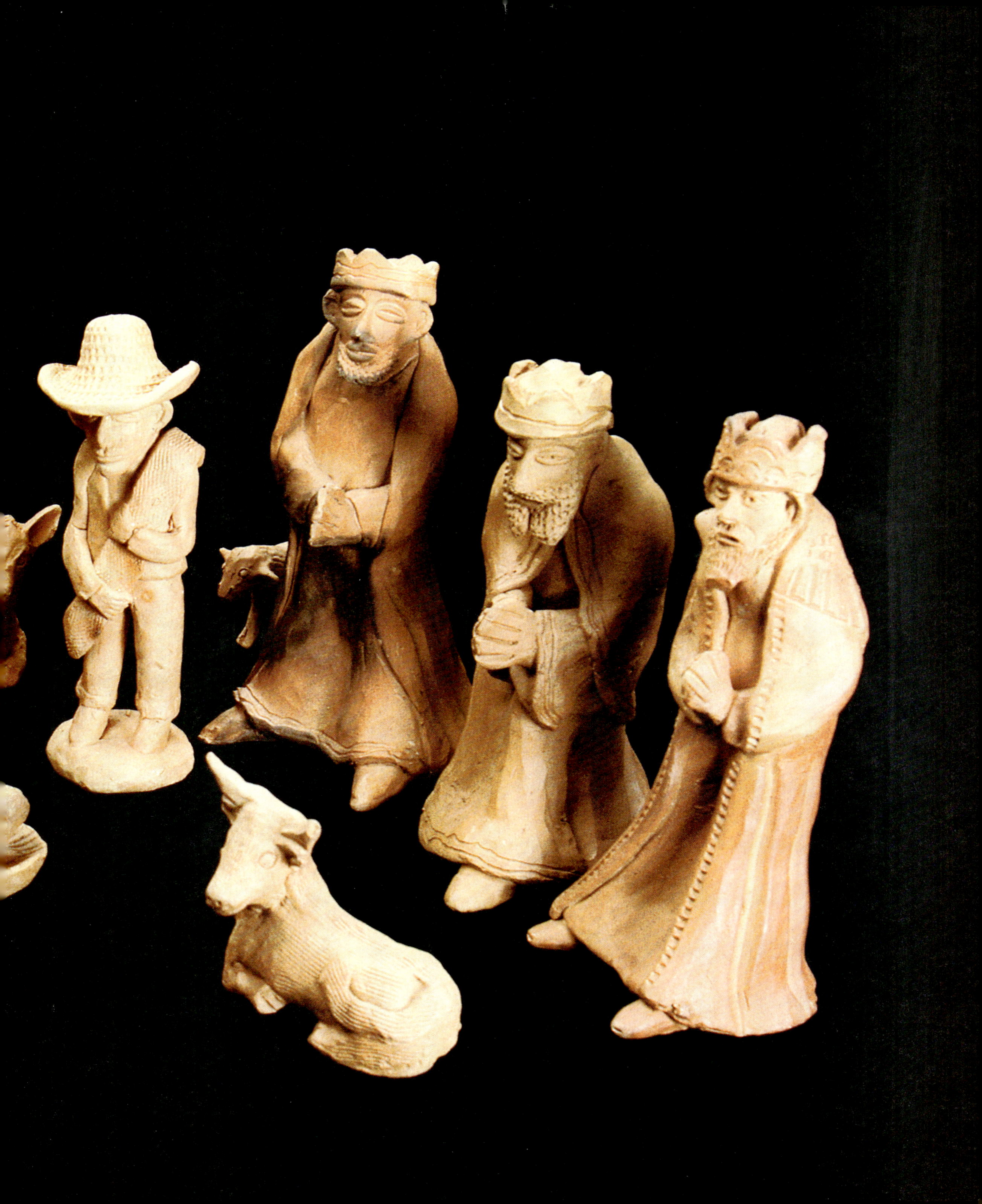

A Danish crèche is a mobile sculpture 2 feet high: heat rising from the lighted candles causes the fan to turn, rotating the three figures.

Contemporary Polish artisans created this highly stylized crèche. The donkey and the cow in this scene are represented only by carved heads.

A crèche from Nigeria is carved out of large thorns that grow on several different kinds of trees native to the country. These interesting folk-art figures are dressed in the costumes that the artist could observe being worn by people around him.

CRÈCHES / 81

For this crèche made in Israel, the Holy Family are depicted as Arabs, and the infant Jesus is being held in his mother's arms rather than in a crib.

MUSEUMS AND LIBRARIES
The Metropolitan Museum of Art
New York, New York 10028

The Regina Laudis Monastery
Bethlehem, Connecticut 06751

BOOKS
De Robeck, Nesta, *The Christmas Crib*. The Bruce Publishing Company, 1956.

Hillier, Mary, *Dolls & Dollmakers*. Weidenfeld and Nicholson, 1968.

Viva Jesús, María, y José: A Celebration of the Birth of Jesus. Trinity University Press, 1977.

Von Boehn, Max, *Puppets and Automata*. Dover Publications, Inc., 1972.

PUBLISHED BY CURRIER & IVES

Currier & Ives
A Heritage in Prints

Nathaniel Currier and James M. Ives, proprietors of the largest lithographic company in the United States during the last half of the 19th Century, were, like most Americans of their time, horse-racing buffs; as a result, it was natural for them to publish approximately 750 different racing prints. Those prints were the ones that started me off as a Currier & Ives collector, since my work involves me in televising horse races.

I was wandering around antique shops in Chicago when it occurred to me to ask if anyone had anything related to harness racing. A few minutes later I paid $80 for a lithograph titled *The Celebrated Horse George M.*

Sidney Alpert, whose company produces video-tape records of horse races, has the largest Currier & Ives collection in private hands.

Patchen—"*The Champion of the Turf.*" That was my first Currier & Ives print.

Since then I have bought many more Currier & Ives lithographs and trade cards on racing as well as on a broad range of subjects, including country views, comic situations, disasters, trains, panoramic vistas, hunting scenes, yacht races, prize fighters, sentimental family groups and craftsmen at work. Currier & Ives described itself as "Publishers of Cheap and Popular Pictures," and the company indeed lived up to the claim. Its mass-produced prints were indeed a popular medium that brought images of the world into the homes of Americans of the middle classes.

The company was prolific—it turned out something on the order of 10 million prints on nearly 10,000 subjects. Today, a print collector can find the work of other lithographers of that time—Endicott & Company (known particularly for pictures of steamboats), Henry

Reporting news of disasters in spectacular lithographs was a specialty of Currier & Ives. This is their depiction of the Great Chicago Fire of 1871, when the heart of the city burned to the ground and some 300 people died. It shows Chicagoans fleeing the flaming city—in improbably orderly rows—across the Randolph Street Bridge.

R. Robinson, Nagel & Weingaertner, Major & Knapp—but as collectibles Currier & Ives prints are as renowned now as they were in the last half of the 19th Century.

At their peak, partners Nathaniel Currier and James Ives did better than their competitors not only because they were highly skilled craftsmen but also because they were diligent merchandisers. The company sold by mail as well as through street vendors and ordinary retail outlets in New York City, where the shop was located. It had travelers selling prints across the country and abroad, in Europe, Australia and in Latin America, where it provided some prints with Spanish titles.

Currier in particular is credited with the popular touch. He had a gift for picking subjects with mass-sales appeal, giving the drawings deft finishing touches and capping his selections by giving the prints winning titles. They appealed to patriotism, to love of family and devotion to home ties as well as reverence for middle-class virtues in general. Titles of sporting prints were sprinkled with glittering words like "champion," "grand," "celebrated" and "magnificent."

Currier got an early start in the business. He was 21 when he opened his own business in New York in 1835, a time when lithography as a printing process was still a relatively new import in the United States. Currier had learned the craft in Boston, where he worked for the first successful American lithographers, William and John Pendleton.

Seventeen years later, in 1852, Currier took on his brother-in-law, James Merritt Ives, as bookkeeper. Eleven years younger than Currier, Ives had artistic leanings as well as business training. He became a partner in 1857, when the imprint was changed from "N. Currier" to "Currier & Ives."

The partners evidently complemented each other in business acumen as they did physically. Currier was spare and fair, Ives rather dumpy and dark. Currier is credited with a good sense of humor and a charming personality. He married twice, and had one son. Ives had two sons and four daughters. He was active in religious and civic enterprises, and was a frequent member of committees that handed out awards for prize-winning art. He too had a good sense of the comic. Both men were gifted with a well-developed instinct for news, and their office was always a lively place that drew visits from such notables as the eminent preacher Henry Ward Beecher, the newspaper editor Horace Greeley and the great promoter P. T. Barnum.

The publishing house run by Currier and Ives for upward of 40 years flourished even after Currier's death in 1888 and Ives's in 1895. By 1907, however, the company had run out of steam under the management of the founders' sons. They did not rise to the challenge of new printing techniques, and the company collapsed.

Many of the prints published by the firm showed the artists' names, and their identification with their pictures adds interest—and value. The most prolific staff artist was probably Mrs. Florence (Fanny) Palmer. At her death in 1876, she had worked for Currier & Ives for at least 25 years. She produced an enormous number of pictures on a variety of subjects, including the cottage and railroad scenes for which the company was particularly famous.

Louis Maurer worked on staff for Currier & Ives from 1852 to about 1862, and then on commission for many years. His best-known works are probably those done for the "Life of a Fireman" *(page 85)* and the "Turf" horse-racing series.

A prolific artist who turned out hundreds of comic prints was Thomas Worth. Worth sold his first picture to Nathaniel Currier by walking in off the street, aged 20, with a picture of an old horse pulling a wagon that was driven by two boys. Currier gave him five dollars for it, a large sum in those days. The picture was altered somewhat and published with the title, *A Brush on the Road, Mile Heats, Best 2 in 3*. Prints of it were bringing about $200 in the 1970s.

Currier & Ives also purchased pieces from such well-

One of Currier & Ives's price lists, a rarity not previously reproduced, quotes the "First Futurity Race at Sheepshead Bay, N.Y." at $6, though many sources state that no print cost more than $3.75 when issued.

established artists as the landscape painter George Inness, cartoonist and illustrator Thomas Nast, and A. F. (Arthur Fitzwilliam) Tait, a leading painter of outdoor life, who was responsible for many of the sporting and hunting prints published by the firm.

The prices Currier & Ives charged for its prints depended partly on size, designated in so-called folio sizes by collectors. A folio, in this usage, is simply a single sheet of paper. "Very small folio" is up to 7 by 9 inches; "small folio" runs from approximately 9 by 14 to 14 by 20 inches; finally there is "large folio," anything larger than 14 by 20 inches—sometimes much larger.

The least expensive small pictures were sold for as little as 20 cents, but prices went up to six dollars for large folios. A century later, the range was much, much greater—from less than $20 to many thousands of dollars. Only the rarest command the highest prices. These include those subjects represented by only a few titles. For example, the subject of whaling is treated in probably no more than 15 titles, and only one ice-boating picture is known. On the other hand, there are more than 700 titles dealing with sentimental subjects such as those shown on pages 94 and 98.

The most valuable of all Currier & Ives is the large folio (approximately 18$\frac{12}{16}$ by 27$\frac{1}{16}$ inches, excluding the margins) *Life of a Hunter—A Tight Fix*, showing a hunter battling an enraged bear in snowy woods. One in fine condition was sold for $8,500 in 1973. The original painting for this 1861 print was done by A. F. Tait, a fact that accounts for much of the value.

Large folio prints cost more because they are usually superior as art: the composition is more fully developed and more detailed, and the coloring is usually better than that of smaller prints.

But it is not necessary to pay large sums for genuine Currier & Ives prints. Among those available in the 1970s for as little as $20 were the small folios with girls' names as their titles. There are more than 250 different pictures in this series, but many bear the same name—Esther, Flora, Eliza, Martha or Mary.

Another affordable Currier & Ives product often overlooked is the postcard-sized trade cards given away by merchants to advertise goods or services. Many of these pictures were simply reduced versions of larger Currier & Ives prints. At least 100 different trade cards are known, some dated 1880. Because many people—both dealers and collectors—are not aware of this part of the Currier & Ives output, examples can sometimes be purchased quite inexpensively.

To understand the aspects of Currier & Ives works that influence their value—and to distinguish originals from fakes or reproductions—you need to know how the prints were made. Two slightly different versions of the same subject may have different titles, otherwise

Currier's lithograph of the burned-out Merchant's Exchange in New York dates from 1835, the year he went into business on his own. His first big seller, it went on sale just four days after the fire.

There is a personal touch to Currier & Ives's "The American Fireman, Prompt to the Rescue." The model for the fire fighter was partner James Ives, who was a volunteer fireman in Brooklyn.

identical prints might vary slightly in size, and so on.

Production of a Currier & Ives print began with an artist who provided original drawings or paintings for a print. A lithographer copied the art with a waxy crayon or ink onto the plate (Currier's brother Charles, as it happens, invented an improved wax crayon), a smooth slab of lithographic stone, preferably porous limestone. Acid then ate away the stone where it was not drawn on, leaving the image in relief. When a grease-based ink was applied to the stone, the ink adhered only to the raised, waxy drawing. A sheet of paper, dampened to make it take ink better, was placed on the stone, which was then rolled through the press. The result was one "impression"—a lithographic print left on the paper. Then the stone was re-inked for another impression.

Although the company's lithographic process produced only a black-and-white image, most Currier & Ives prints were designed to be published in color. Some small prints were sold in black and white, or "plain," and are less desirable.

For those prints that were colored, an assembly-line procedure was used for all but the large ones. About twelve young women (working for a penny a print) brushed on watercolors. Each woman was assigned one color. Following a colored model set in the middle of their worktable, each colored in those parts that received her color and then passed the print on to her neighbor. The large pictures were sent out in batches to artists who did all the coloring work for each. Some got one dollar per batch.

Such hand-colored prints have continuous tones, essentially indistinguishable from hand-drawn artwork. Modern reproductions of Currier & Ives are done photographically, usually by a method that breaks the tones into tiny dots visible with a magnifying glass.

However, some fakes have been produced by the old continuous-tone process and reveal no giveaway dots. My first test of any print is to examine the paper. Currier & Ives used a very heavy, strong paper, almost pure white in color—no beige or gray tinge—and generally resistant to stains. Fakes are usually made on flimsier, slightly tinted stock.

A further clue to authenticity is the dimensions of the paper. The damp paper on which Currier & Ives lithographs were printed shrank as it dried, and because the amount of shrinking varied, the actual sizes of the finished prints vary slightly. Genuine prints should be close to the original dimensions—listed for each subject in reference books *(page 99)*—but they may vary in size somewhat because of the variation in shrinkage.

Currier & Ives did not make limited editions. They printed as many copies as they thought the market would absorb, and as many as could be printed from an individual stone before it "broke down"—that is, could no longer provide a clear impression. If the stone for a very popular seller broke down, it was polished smooth

THE EXPRESS TRAIN.

Though railroading pictures like "The Express Train" (above) were popular, the firm made only about 40 prints on this subject. As a result such lithographs are rare and valuable. The company did five versions of "The Express Train," varying the number of cars and other details.

with sand and the image was redrawn. Subsequent editions of the print were sometimes given a different title, possibly for copyright reasons, so that a collector today might find two almost identical prints with different titles. Both could be genuine. It is believed that tens of thousands of the most popular prints were pulled, but unfortunately no production records exist.

Condition is crucial in determining the value of Currier & Ives prints. Even though many of the prints are more than 100 years old, copies exist unstained, unripped and untrimmed. This last condition is very important—a print without margins, one that has been trimmed to fit a frame, is next to worthless as a collectible. A print in less than perfect condition because it has some stains or rips can be fairly well repaired by a professional. But trimmed margins are unrestorable. If you are tempted to buy a print that has been framed, insist that the seller show you that the frame hides no imperfections or trimming.

Since so many genuine Currier & Ives prints were produced in the 19th Century, you might imagine surviving examples to be everywhere. They are not, but there are a number of good sources. Antique dealers and art galleries handle them, but at high, if not top, prices. I have had better experiences in small antique or curiosity shops. Secondhand shops and charity outlets sometimes have framed prints hanging on the walls above the furniture and old overcoats. They are worth checking, for occasionally one turns out to be an unrecognized but authentic Currier & Ives original. Other inexpensive places to look are frame shops and secondhand bookstores in small towns.

I have also made good buys at auctions, particularly at country sales where prints may come on the block between farm machinery and bedclothes and slip through largely unnoticed. After I began collecting seriously I became a familiar figure at certain regularly held auctions. Everyone was soon bidding strongly against me because they assumed I knew which items were really valuable. That is one disadvantage in being known. I stopped going to auctions myself and sent a friend instead. Over the years my Currier & Ives collection outgrew my home. Unfortunately, I now have to keep most of the prints in storage.

An advantage I have found in being known as a serious collector is that private owners and dealers will often call me when they are about to sell special prints. But this does not mean that I get any special treatment on prices. So even when I am offered something I really want, I do not hesitate to ask, "Would you do a little better on the price?"

For related material, see the articles on Botanical Prints, Cartoons & Caricatures, Japanese Prints, Magazines, Maps, Posters, and Trade Cards in separate volumes of The Encyclopedia of Collectibles.

A gruesome nautical incident provided a Currier subject in 1842, when three crew members on the brig-of-war "Somers" were hanged after being charged with mutiny. Two bodies can be seen at left.

88 / CURRIER & IVES

"The Celebrated Horse Lexington" (left) is valued because few copies exist and the subject was a famous thoroughbred stud in its day.

This 1869 lithograph of a busy blacksmith shop is a much sought-after Currier & Ives. The workings of the smithy are pictured in close detail, from the bellows used to raise the heat of the forge to the precisely drawn prints on the wall—no doubt by Currier & Ives.

CURRIER & IVES / 89

GREAT HORSES IN A GREAT RACE.
SALVATOR AND TENNY.

Horse racing was the people's sport in the 19th Century, and Currier & Ives specialized in pictures on this subject, portraying virtually every major race and recording full results in the titles. This print is noted for its documentation of the role of black jockeys in American racing.

In an 1882 portrait, the record-breaking pacer Little Brown Jug, after whom the most renowned pacing event is named, pulls an old-fashioned high-wheeled sulky.

The Pacing Wonder **LITTLE BROWN JUG,** *of Chicago, Ills.*
RECORD 2:11¾.

THE SPIRIT OF THE UNION.

Lo! on high the glorious form,
Of WASHINGTON lights all the gloom,
And words of warning seem to come;
From out the portal of his tomb.

Americans, your fathers shed,
Their blood to rear the UNIONS fame,
Then let your blood as free be given,
The bond of UNION to maintain.

This patriotic print issued in 1860 depicts George Washington, his tomb and Mount Vernon, his home, as well as the national Capitol.

CURRIER & IVES / 91

The "Battle at Bunker's Hill" is based on the celebrated painting by Colonel John Trumbull. The marginal sketches picture some of the participants.

An undated print, "The Star Spangled Banner," shows the flag displayed by an allegorical figure depicting American Liberty.

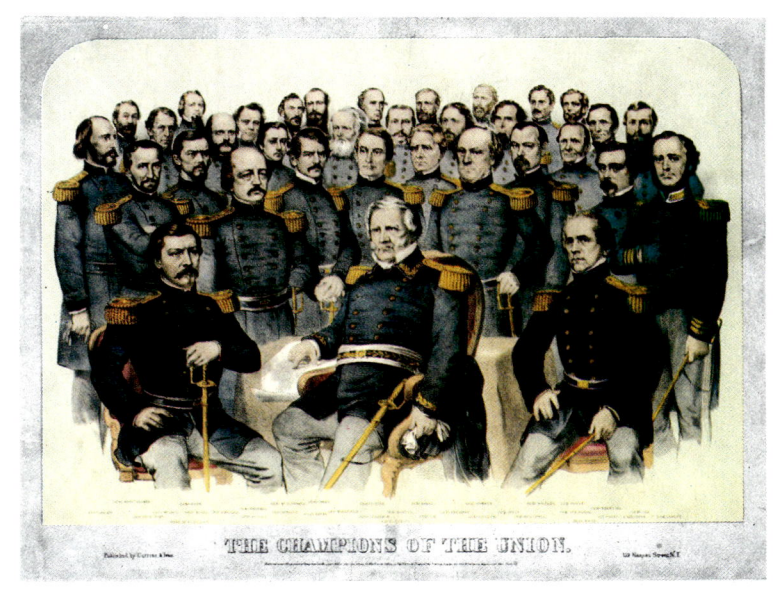

"The Champions of the Union" portrays 25 Civil War officers, including (seated) Generals Winfield Scott, George McClellan and John E. Wool.

President William Henry Harrison died in 1841 soon after this print went into production; a black border was added for mourning.

92 / CURRIER & IVES

During the Civil War, thousands of prints of the fighting were turned out. Currier & Ives's battle scenes, like this view of a Union success near Richmond, were stylized and, as might be expected, depicted Union troops triumphant.

MALVERN HILL, VA. JULY 1ST 1862.

"The Four Seasons of Life: Middle Age" (above) is one of five in an 1868 series. Artist James Ives, in showing a Currier & Ives print on the wall in a middle-class American home, was being an accurate reporter.

This version of "Preparing for Market" is one of four of the subject done in 1856. Here a toy horse stands by the porch. In others a child is shown, with and without the toy; still another version has neither child nor toy.

CURRIER & IVES / 95

SKATING SCENE—MOONLIGHT.

Moonlit skating on a lake is the subject of one of many prints of winter activities. Sports and travel scenes involving snow and ice were favored equally by the partners and their customers. This print was done in 1868.

THE ROAD,—WINTER.

"The Road—Winter" was created by company employees as a surprise Christmas present for Nathaniel Currier and his wife, who are portrayed in the sleigh. Currier liked the print so much he added it to the inventory.

96 / CURRIER & IVES

THE VELOCIPEDE.

Currier & Ives reported new fads. Here a bicycle is shown in the act of proving the slogan, "We can beat the swiftest steed...."

FASHIONABLE "TURN-OUTS" IN CENTRAL PARK.

A high-society scene in New York's Central Park includes fashionably turned-out riders in an open calèche (foreground) and a brougham (center).

CURRIER & IVES / 97

AMERICAN HUNTING SCENES.

An 1863 wilderness print is based on an A. F. Tait painting, perhaps one made at his hunting camp in the Adirondacks, where he often worked.

Artist Fanny Palmer drew this 1866 print, regarded as the firm's most attractive game picture. It has sold for more than $7,000.

THE HAPPY FAMILY.

98 / CURRIER & IVES

THE WOODLAND GATE.

"The Woodland Gate," undated, focuses on the innocent joys of childhood, a subject treated in many ways by Currier & Ives.

KITTIES AMONG THE ROSES.

Baby animals and flowers were popular subjects, and the print above of kittens with roses is among the many to combine both.

LIGHT ARTILLERY.

The sentimental scene of "Light Artillery" was based on an 1863 painting by Thomas Nast, famed political cartoonist.

THE CITY OF WASHINGTON.

Lithographers found a ready market for bird's-eye views of American cities, and Currier and Ives were leading practitioners of the art. The firm brought out its largest-known folio in this view of Washington, D.C., in 1880. It shows the city as viewed from the Potomac.

MUSEUMS AND LIBRARIES
Boston Public Library
Boston, Massachusetts 02117

Library of Congress
Washington, D.C. 20540

Museum of the City of New York
Harry T. Peters Collection
New York, New York 10029

Museum of Fine Arts
Boston, Massachusetts 02115

New York Public Library
New York, New York 10018

Philadelphia Museum of Art
Philadelphia, Pennsylvania 19101

COLLECTORS ORGANIZATIONS
American Historical Print Collectors Society, Inc.
P.O. Box 962
Westbury, New York 11590

PERIODICALS
Print Collector's Newsletter, New York, New York 10021

BOOKS
Conningham, Frederic A.:
Currier & Ives Prints, An Illustrated Checklist. Crown Publishers, Inc., 1970.
Currier & Ives, 19th Century Printmakers to the American People. Heritage Plantation of Sandwich, 1973.

Peters, Harry T., *Currier & Ives: Printmakers to the American People,* 2 vols. Doubleday, Doran and Co., 1931.

Zigrosser, Carl, and Christa Gaehde, *A Guide to the Collecting and Care of Original Prints.* Crown Publishers, Inc., 1973.

Cut Glass
Wares that Sparkle like Diamonds

A valuable pitcher called a tankard is in the Aztec pattern, which has side design elements, or motifs, known as chains—rows top to bottom of "hobstars" alternating with narrower rows of "cane buttons."

A fountain 17 feet high and made entirely of glittering cut glass was ooh'd and ah'd over by millions of visitors to the Centennial Exposition of 1876 in Philadelphia. Of the 43 American glass companies represented at the show, fewer than 10 exhibited cut glass, but their displays set off a cut-glass fad. Within a few decades several hundred makers were busily supplying similar glassware, for a piece of showy cut glass became the prized anniversary or wedding gift for countless Americans around the turn of the century.

The style that was made popular at the Centennial is elaborate, consisting of patterns made up of design ele-

---

Lamar Landfair, who is in the lumber business, bought his first piece of cut glass in 1953. His collection includes more than 225 pieces of cut glass—American "brilliant" wares as well as engraved glass.

---

ments called motifs *(page 105)*. It is known as brilliant—an apt name, for these wares sparkle almost like diamonds. This effect is achieved by making deep cuts with a large abrasive wheel in a glass blank, then polishing the glass. Deep cutting is made possible by the use of a kind of glass called flint, lead glass or simply crystal. The technical term for the glass is "soft," a condition achieved by adding red lead to the basic ingredients.

Originally the polishing was done on a wooden wheel with pumice or jeweler's rouge. After 1900 an acid dip was used before, or sometimes instead of, the polishing step in order to save time. Acid polishing does not produce results equal to those of handwork, and an increasing reliance on the use of acid was one factor in a decrease in quality and a gradual decline in the popularity of brilliant cut glass. The most sought-after pieces are thus the brilliants made between 1876 and World War I. However, collectors like myself value many kinds of glassware produced with a small abrasive wheel, some cut with simple designs in Europe and America beginning in the 1700s, others more delicately decorated by engraving, and still others combining several styles.

When the brilliant style was most popular, manufac-

These glasses from the 1890s are in the intricate Wedgemere pattern. Deep, V-shaped "miter" cuts are clearly seen in the bowl of the champagne glass (far right), crossing below the round hobstar in the center.

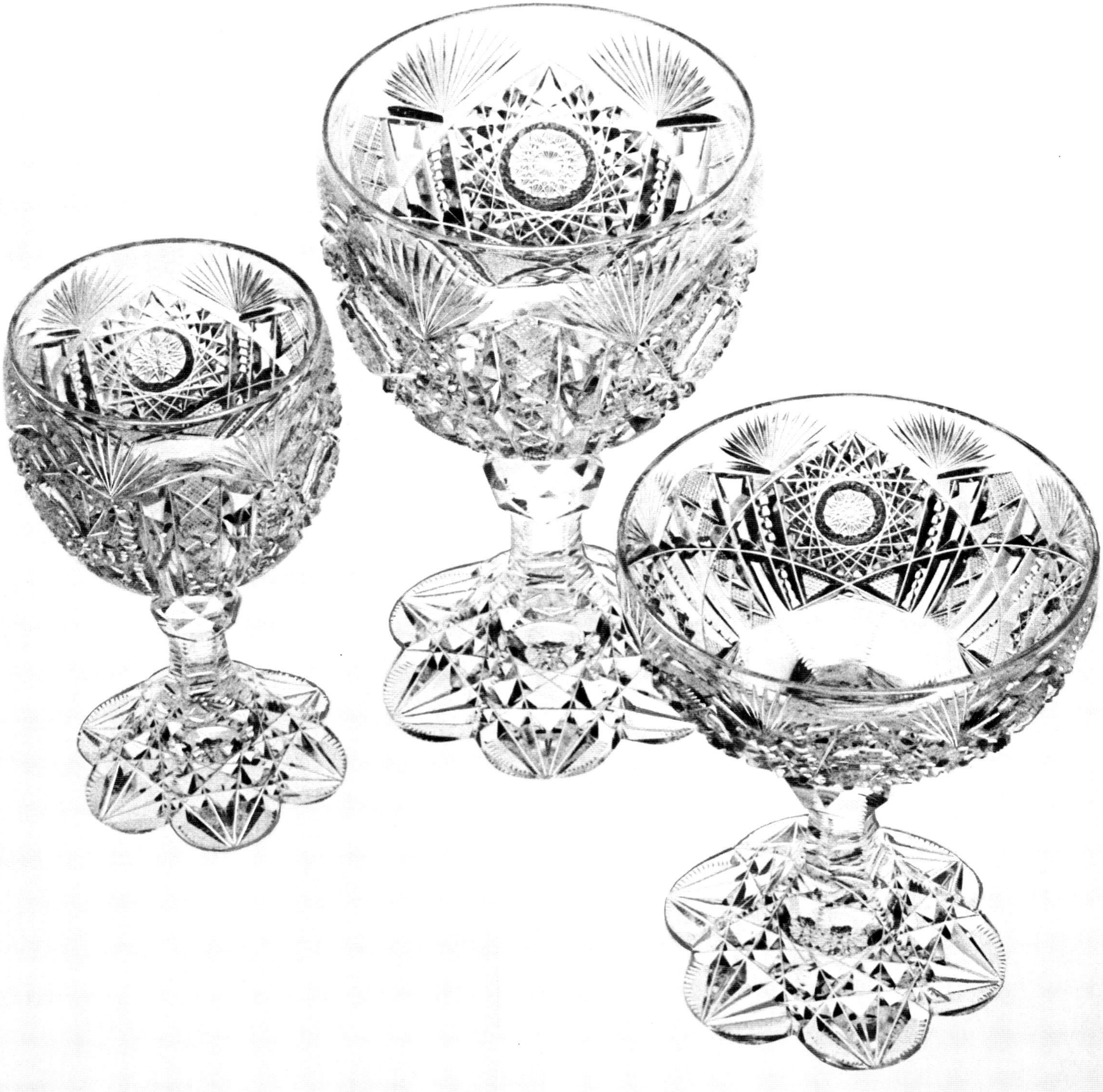

This loving cup has a third handle, out of sight on the far side, in addition to the two visible ones—a design commonly used for glass loving cups in the late 19th Century.

A cut-glass basket 14 inches tall was made in two pieces: the handle was produced separately and later attached to the elaborately cut bowl. It and the piece at top were produced by the Libbey Glass Company.

turers put out cut-glass versions of practically anything that could be made of glass—plates, bowls, vases, cups and saucers, pitchers and other serving pieces. As collectibles, everyday household wares naturally have less value than unusual pieces—three-handled loving cups *(page 102)* and clocks *(page 104).* Also valuable are any colored pieces *(pages 112-113),* and custom-made pieces, generally inscribed, made for an exhibition or special occasion. Many of the custom-made pieces thought to be unique probably are not: companies often made two of anything ordered, in case of damage during shipping.

Because condition is a major concern in cut glass, I buy only pristine pieces without cracks, and without flakes or chips in rim or bases. To avoid damaged pieces that have been "repaired" by being ground down, look closely at the pattern to see that the motifs are complete—that the points of stars or sunbursts are not cut off, that flowers and leaves are whole and that no design runs into the edge. You can test for invisible cracks by listening to the sound the glass makes when tapped. Crystal has a characteristic ringing tone when lightly flicked with a finger. The sound is deadened by a crack, so always ask if you can tap before you buy.

Mismated pieces are another problem. You may be offered tumblers whose motifs differ slightly from those of the pitcher they are being sold with. Another common mismatch occurs with decanters and stoppers. In this case the factory practice of scratching a number on the stopper to match a number on the neck of the decanter will help you. Some dealers think that any stopper is better than none, and they supply mismated stoppers not so much to defraud as to please.

To most collectors, positive identification of a piece—by pattern and maker—is important. Although there were hundreds of producers, some of whom manufactured glass and then cut it, while others simply operated small shops cutting glass blanks that they bought elsewhere, only a few turned out the pieces now prized.

Some American brilliant cut glass can be identified by makers' marks. I did not discover marks until five years after I had bought my first piece. I was looking at a small bowl in a shop one day when the dealer commented, "That's signed." He showed me how to tilt the piece this way and that until I could see a mark on the inside bottom. Marks *(page 103)* were etched by applying acid to the glass with a small rubber stamp. Look for them on the inside centers of shallow bowls and plates; the edges of the bases of bottles and decanters; and near the handles, the inside centers, or the edges of the bases of pitchers and other handled pieces. Use a magnifying glass and an oblique light source—a flashlight is helpful.

Inexpensive imitations of cut glass are common. The real thing always shows sharpness in the cuts, particularly in the "miter," or V-shaped, cuts that mark the major

CUT-GLASS MAKERS' MARKS

Below are some of the marks that were used to identify the wares of leading manufacturers of brilliant cut glass in the United States, several of them located in the glassmaking center of Corning, New York. The marks of Libbey Glass Company and T. G. Hawkes & *Company, the most prolific producers, are the ones most often found. Not all important glassmaking companies used identifying marks; one that generally did not was C. Dorflinger & Sons, located in White Mills, Pennsylvania.*

M. J. AVERBECK NEW YORK CITY	J. D. BERGEN COMPANY MERIDEN, CONNECTICUT	T. B. CLARK & COMPANY HONESDALE, PENNSYLVANIA	T. G. HAWKES & COMPANY CORNING, NEW YORK
J. HOARE & COMPANY CORNING, NEW YORK	LIBBEY GLASS COMPANY TOLEDO, OHIO	H.P. SINCLAIRE & COMPANY CORNING, NEW YORK	TUTHILL CUT GLASS COMPANY MIDDLETOWN, NEW YORK

divisions of the pattern. The imitations, which are usually pressed, or cut on a pressed blank rather than one blown by hand, give themselves away by the rounded edges in the cuts. Even when examined with the naked eye, imitation cut glass will appear somewhat worn.

Although now I buy most of my pieces from dealers, I also check the classifieds in local newspapers for notices of flea markets and yard sales where unexpected bargains may be waiting—even if, as I usually find, the sellers know the market value of every piece they offer.

Once I found an ad that led me to imagine an old lady sadly selling the contents of her large home before moving into smaller quarters. On arriving I found a woman in a house full of junk and mediocre antiques. Mixed with some battered old cut glass were new European vases and bowls, cut in the brilliant manner but easily distinguished from genuine old American wares because the cutting was smooth, having been cheaply finished with an acid dip. I left quickly.

A week later I fell for another of her ads—the setting now was a trailer park; the junk was the same. There were two more misleading ads, the last for a sale at a run-down farmhouse out in the country. Thereafter I figured that I could intuitively spot her ads, and ignore them. But there is a nagging doubt each time I think I see one: "What if this time it's *not* her?"

For related material, see the articles on Depression Glass in this volume, and on Art Glass, Carnival Glass and Pressed Glass in separate volumes of this encyclopedia.

T. G. Hawkes & Company made this whiskey jug, 9 inches high. It is in the Chrysanthemum pattern, one of the most desired in the deeply cut brilliant style, and a grand-prize winner at the 1889 Paris Exposition.

104 / CUT GLASS

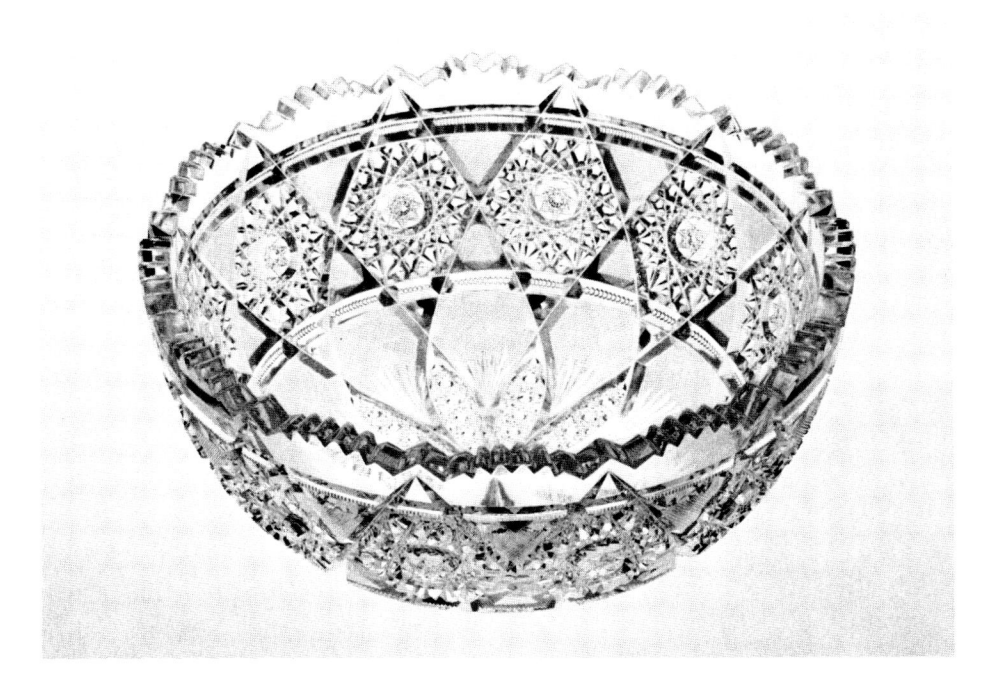

A bowl in the Rex pattern, now extremely rare, won a gold medal for the Tuthill Cut Glass Company at the Panama Pacific Exposition, held in 1915 in San Francisco.

Fine jewelry stores offered clocks in cut-glass cases like this one. The dome is in the subtle silver-thread pattern—close and fine cuts— with an engraved medallion on the side.

The "Brilliant" Motifs

The patterns of cut glass from the brilliant period—1876 to about the beginning of World War I—are composed of several design elements, or motifs. The overall pattern of a piece has no fewer than two motifs, generally an elaborate major motif and one or more minor ones. Some of the motifs were adapted from the traditional designs that were used earlier in Europe and America to make engraved glassware and other styles of cut glass.

Collectors identify pieces by citing the pattern name and also the motifs that are combined to make up the pattern. Several of the motifs most commonly used are pictured in the illustrations at right. The pictures below are details, showing distinctive motifs used in making up patterns that are rare and avidly sought.

The motif most often used is the round hobstar, with a raised, cut center. Deep intersecting lines form eight to 32 star "points" around the edge. This pattern has 24.

Crosshatching, a motif used to fill in an area with tiny light-reflecting facets, is visible on either side of the cane motif, so named for its resemblance to chair caning.

The most common variant of the Russian pattern has "buttons" (three are visible at center) surrounded by lines that intersect, forming two starlike "daisies" on each side.

The Harvard pattern alternates rows of buttons (center) similar to those used in the Russian pattern at left with another type of button made up of crosshatching.

Rosettes—hobstar motif variations—are set off here by wide, deep interwoven cuts, a basketweave motif given no special name. The two motifs form the Trellis pattern.

106 / CUT GLASS

This punch bowl with a separate base is in the Trellis pattern of rosettes and interwoven stripes, shown in detail on page 105. Fifteen inches high and 16 inches across, the bowl is by the O. F. Egginton Company.

A 12-inch decanter was made by T. B. Clark & Company in a pattern known as Quatrefoil and Rosette. Centered on the bowl of the decanter is a hobstar medallion with what is called a rose-cut diamond center.

With an unmistakable horseshoe and a simple four-leaf clover, the pattern of this dish is called, not surprisingly, Good Luck. The piece was cut by the J. D. Bergen Company.

A rare decanter 12 inches tall is decorated with subtly shaded birds and leaves created by engraving, a process that produces the design with a small abrasive wheel instead of the larger wheel used to make the deep, bold incisions of brilliant cut glass. The decanter is believed to be the work of Joseph Haselbauer, an exceptionally gifted engraver associated with J. Hoare & Company.

Masterworks from Europe

The brilliant style of deeply cut glass never became as popular in Europe as it did in America, but fine wares in other styles were made during the 19th Century in many countries. Quantities were imported into the United States then as now, to the delight of modern collectors who find many beautiful examples surviving.

Among the most famous European glassmakers—many of whom marked their work—were Val Saint Lambert of Belgium, Harrachov and Riedel of Bohemia, Stevens & Williams and Thomas Webb & Sons of England, Baccarat and Saint-Louis of France, J. & L. Lobmeyr of Vienna and a number of Irish firms, all of whose products have since come to be called Waterford.

Ireland became a glass center in the early 19th Century because English firms moved their factories there to escape restrictive taxes at home; when the tax laws were changed, glassmaking revived in England and virtually died out in Ireland—it was reestablished a century later, after World War II, by the modern Waterford company, which is not related to its 19th Century predecessors.

Some of the glass produced in Europe can be distinguished by its material. Irish and certain English products have a smoky tint, while German and Bohemian wares were made of "soda" glass that appears to be yellow when viewed under an ultraviolet "black light" lamp, such as the type that mineral collectors use.

But the major characteristics that help identify pieces are the styles associated with each region—although there was much copying back and forth between countries, as well as between Europe and America. Nearly all of the European wares were engraved or cut with a relatively small abrasive wheel, rather than deeply cut with the large wheels used for the brilliant style. If the glass was left unpolished after engraving, the result was soft and shaded *(below)*. If the design was polished, it appeared sharp and bright, as in the example of "rock crystal" at right.

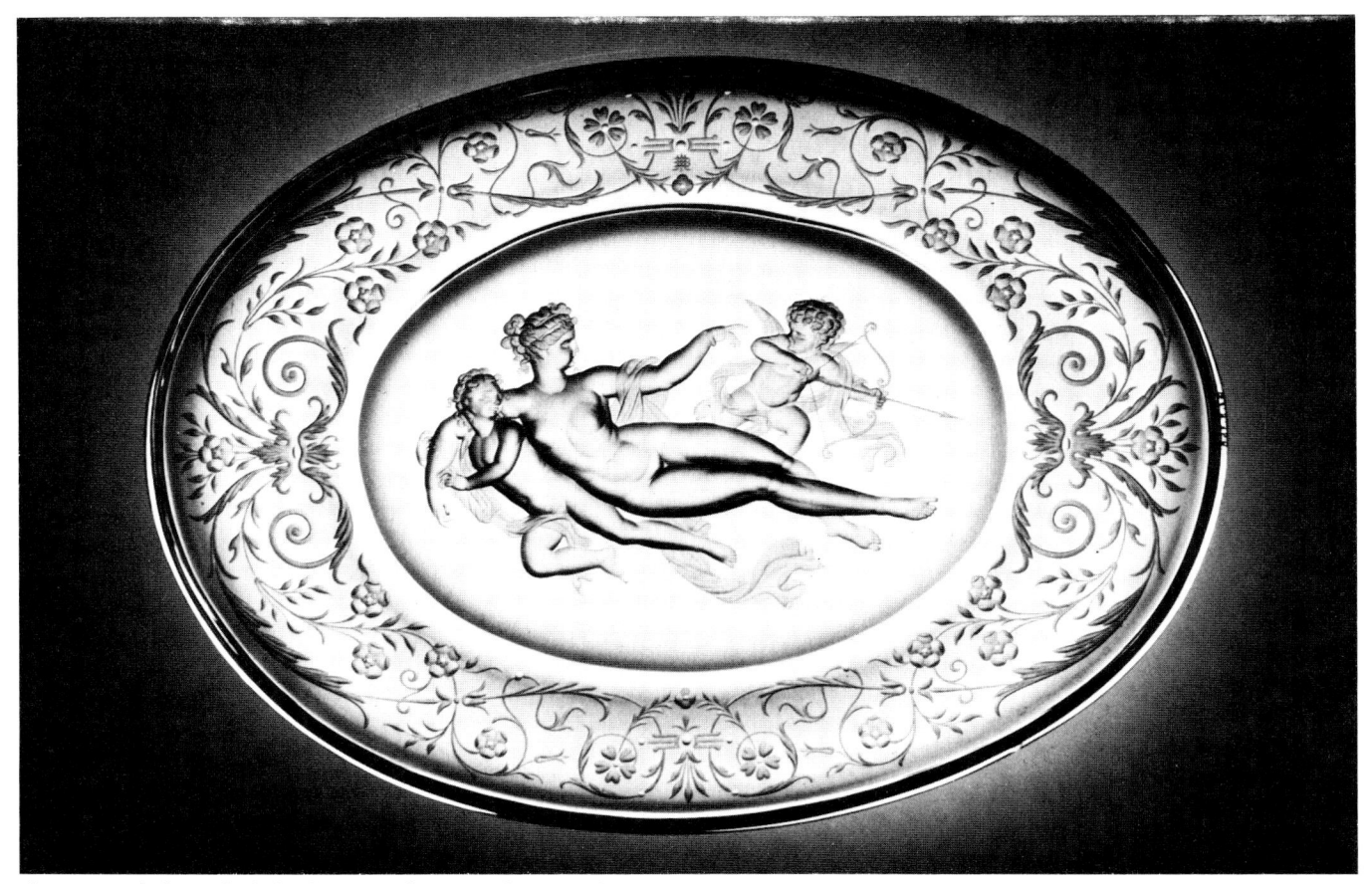

An engraved platter depicting Venus and two cupids is one of a series that was produced by the Viennese firm of J. & L. Lobmeyr.

An English goblet, in the rock-crystal style developed in Bohemia, is signed by William Fritsche, a Bohemian-trained craftsman who worked for a leading English glassmaker, Thomas Webb & Sons of Stourbridge.

A decanter made in Ireland between 1810 and 1815 typifies the style that became known as Waterford. It has a wide pouring lip, neck rings, a rounded body, ribbing, and the design called pillar and arch.

110 / CUT GLASS

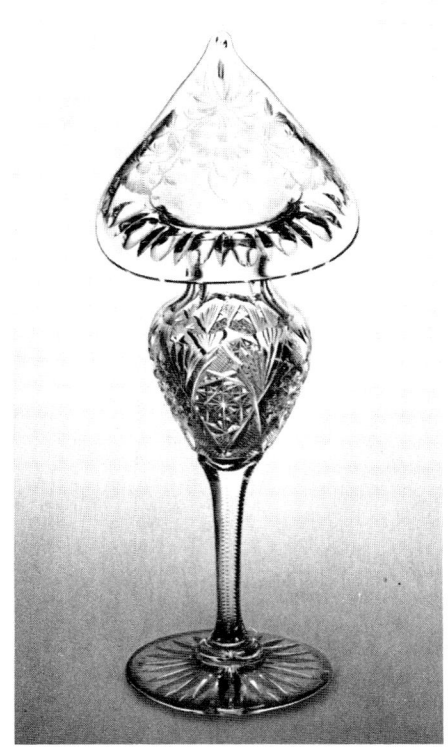

A so-called jack-in-the-pulpit vase has hobstars, fans and strawberry diamonds among many cut-glass motifs, plus engraved flowers.

On a bell made in the Marlboro pattern, the fan motif appears below both sides of the eight-pointed hobstars in the center.

The Plymouth pattern—including hobstars, rosettes and fans—was used for both the pendant-hung shade and the base of the lamp above, one of few made. This one, electric and 21 inches tall, was expensive new—$300 in 1905—and valued at 10 times that figure by a dealer in the 1970s.

CUT GLASS / 111

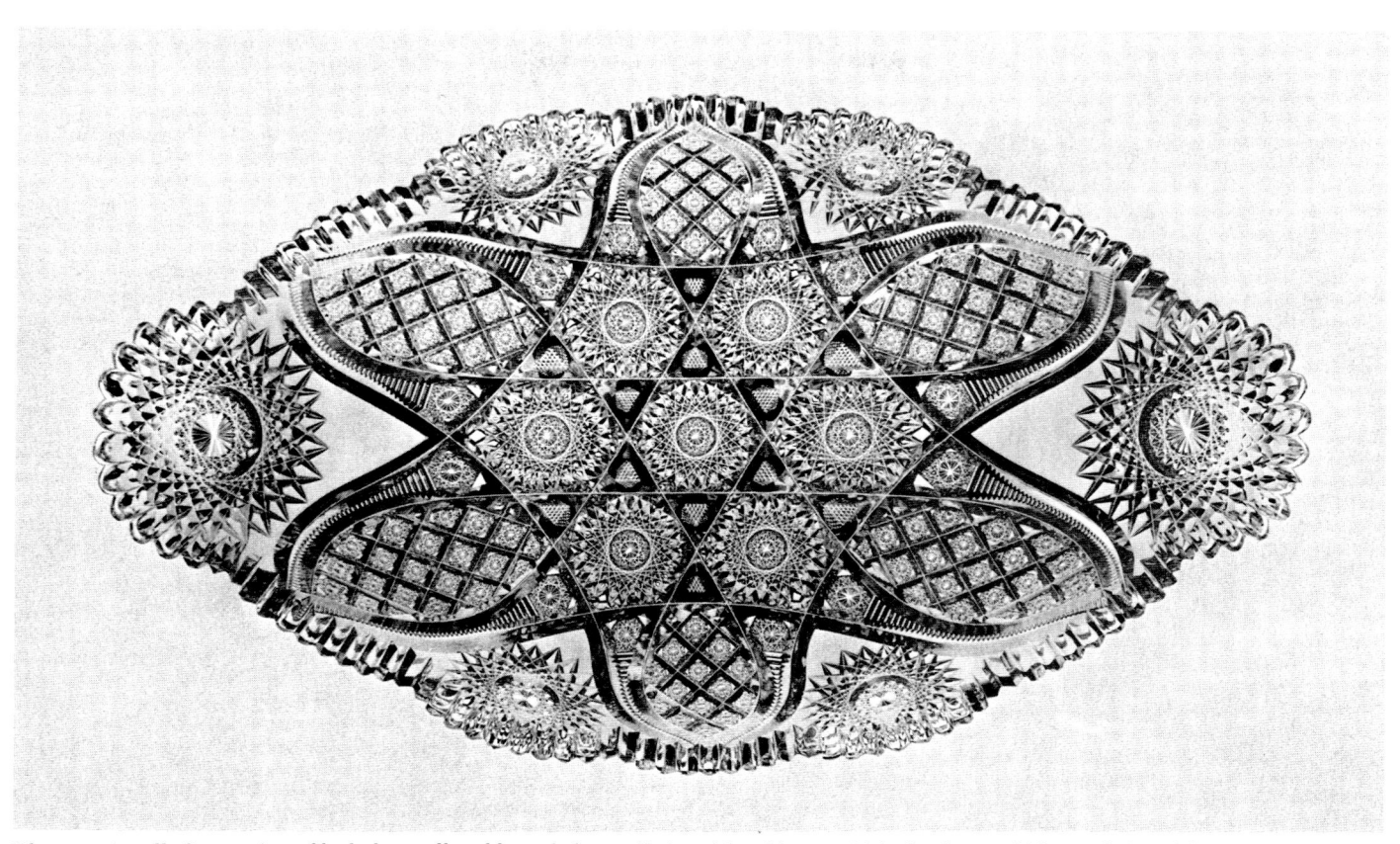

The exceptionally fine cutting of both the small and large hobstars distinguishes this tray, 18 inches long, which was designed for serving ice cream.

The design of this piece is delicately cut in multiple motifs, including hobstars, caning, diamonds and fans. Its purpose is unusual: it is a cuspidor, meant for the well-appointed home of the turn of the century.

Anticipating the 1910 return of Halley's comet, designers found that the customary decorative elements of cut glass lent themselves effectively to depicting a comet in a shallow 8-inch bowl.

112 / CUT GLASS

This gold bowl once belonged to Julien de Cordova, president of the Union Glass Company. Unlike most colored pieces—clear glass overlaid with colored glass before cutting—this one is solid. Colored cut glass is the rarest find because it was usually custom-made.

A perfume bottle 6 inches high displays the two-color effect called cut to clear—motifs cut through an overlay of colored glass to reveal clear glass beneath.

Early-20th Century glasses, apparently intended for Rhine wine, are cranberry cut to clear and green cut to clear. Each was elaborately cut in a variation of the Arcadia pattern and given a "teardrop" in the stem.

Because this 10-inch vase in the Croesus pattern is cranberry cut to clear, it is worth at least twice as much as a clear version of the same piece would be.

CUT GLASS / 113

These four glasses are in the Russian pattern, which is clearly visible at the top of the far side of each. A glass-bubble teardrop can be seen at the top of each stem. In clear versions without the teardrop, such glasses were worth a little more than $100 each in the 1970s. The teardrop adds about a third to the value. Amber or turquoise color adds another third, while cranberry or blue adds a half.

MUSEUMS

Chrysler Museum at Norfolk
Norfolk, Virginia 23510

The Corning Museum of Glass
Corning, New York 14830

Historical Society of Western Pennsylvania
Pittsburgh, Pennsylvania 15213

Lightner Museum
St. Augustine, Florida 32084

The Metropolitan Museum of Art
New York, New York 10028

Philadelphia Museum of Art
Philadelphia, Pennsylvania 19101

The Toledo Museum of Art
Toledo, Ohio 45697

COLLECTORS ORGANIZATIONS

The National Early American Glass Club
55 Cliff Road
Wellesley Hills, Massachusetts 02181

BOOKS

Boggess, Bill and Louise, *American Brilliant Cut Glass*. Crown Publishers, Inc., 1977.

Daniel, Dorothy, *Cut and Engraved Glass, 1771-1905*. William Morrow & Co., Inc., 1967.

Elville, E. M., *English and Irish Cut Glass*. Country Life Limited, 1953.

Evers, Jo, *The Standard Cut Glass Value Guide*. Collector Books, 1975.

Pearson, J. Michael and Dorothy, *American Cut Glass for the Discriminating Collector*. Published by the authors, Box 2844, Miami Beach, Florida 33140, 1965.

Polak, Ada, *Glass, Its Tradition and Its Makers*. G. P. Putnam's Sons, 1975.

Revi, Albert C., *American Cut and Engraved Glass*. Thomas Nelson Inc., 1970.

Schrijver, Elka, *Glass and Crystal*. Universe Books, Inc., 1964.

Schroeder, Bill, *Collectors Illustrated Price Guide Cut Glass*. Collector Books, 1977.

Warren, Phelps, *Irish Glass*. Charles Scribner's Sons, 1970.

Weiss, Gustav, *Books of Glass*. Praeger Publishers, Inc., 1971.

Wiener, Herbert, and Freda Lipkowitz, *Rarities in American Cut Glass*. The Collectors House of Books Publishing Co., 1975.

Vera Fokina
Michael Fokin
„Scheherazade"

Dance Memorabilia
Tokens of an Elusive Art

When I took a year's sabbatical from the university where I teach dance and dance history, it was a busman's holiday. I traveled abroad to look for dance memorabilia. Naturally I included the Soviet Union in my itinerary; after all, it is the homeland of some of the world's leading ballet companies as well as the birthplace and training ground of many of the world's most famous dancers and choreographers, past and present.

One day, while I was browsing through an interesting bookstore during my visit to Leningrad, I suddenly felt someone's hand upon my shoulder. That is not a par-

---
George Verdak, who teaches dance at Butler University in Indianapolis, performed with the Ballet Russe de Monte Carlo. He has collected thousands of pieces of dance memorabilia—many bought while on tour.

---

ticularly pleasant experience in Russia. But when I turned around I saw to my relief one of the bookstore clerks. He beckoned to me. I followed him. In another section of the store he pointed to a shelf that contained a group of Imperial Theatre Yearbooks—lavishly printed, illustrated chronicles of all the productions that were staged by the Ballet Russe.

Two of the gray-bound volumes were even more impressive than the others. They covered the 1899-1900 season, produced under the supervision of Serge Diaghilev, the towering impresario of Russian opera and ballet in the early decades of this century. To me these books were a find with a personal meaning as well as an exciting collecting discovery, for I had worked with several of Diaghilev's dancers when I took part in American tours of the Ballet Russe de Monte Carlo.

The tours had seemed to be interminable—extended train trips kept us on the road for 48 weeks a year. During my nine years with the company, I formed the habit of visiting bookstores and antique shops wherever we performed to look for dance objects, not just mementos of theatrical troupes but also material related to social dancing, since professional and nonprofessional dancing have always been interrelated. I found posters,

One of the many picture postcards depicting dancers, this choice example shows Michel Fokine and his wife Vera in a scene from a production of "Schéhérazade" for which Fokine did the choreography.

A rare mid-19th Century playbill, once posted outside a New York opera house, advertises two plays—and two ballets, one of which, "Giselle," is still in the repertoire of many companies the world over.

115

This poster links four names that add interest: Joan Miró, the Spanish surrealist who designed the poster; Martha Graham, the choreographer; and Margot Fonteyn and Rudolf Nureyev, stars of classical ballet.

Pablo Picasso, who did much work related to ballet early in his career, designed costumes for the Ballet Russe's "Parade," staged in 1917. Above is his sketch for the costume of that production's Chinese conjurer.

programs, moralistic tracts denouncing ballroom dancing, society-ball dance cards, and prints picturing European ballerinas such as Fanny Elssler, who electrified American audiences in the 1840s. (When Elssler performed in the nation's capital, she was received by President Van Buren, and Congress was recessed on the evenings she danced—for lack of a quorum, according to some accounts.)

As the Ballet Russe de Monte Carlo made its annual stops for performances I regularly asked shop owners in each of the cities to remember me whenever they received anything they thought I might be particularly interested in. Before long their notes would arrive in the mail. One said, "I've got a lithograph of Marie Taglioni"; another reported, "We've just received the sheet music for 'The Black Crook.'"

I built up good connections by corresponding with—and, every once in a while, by ordering from—dealers located overseas. It is not necessary, however, to go abroad for valuable dance memorabilia—or even to the center of professional dancing in the United States, New York City. While the European capitals and New York are extremely rich sources, Americans everywhere have long provided appreciative audiences for ballet. As a result the United States has a rich heritage in dance, one that is more widespread than people imagine and that has created a correspondingly diverse store of collectibles. One of the country's notable collections of dance memorabilia, for example, is located in the Public Library of Birmingham, Alabama, the outgrowth of a 1967 donation from a dance patron of that city, Mrs. Catherine Hammond Collins.

Similar mementos of the dance can be discovered just about anywhere in the United States because of the wide-ranging tours of famous performers. As long ago as the 1850s, for example, one of the great dance families of all time, headed by Cesare Cecchetti and including son Enrico—later a teacher whose pupils included

A poster by costume designer and painter Willy Pogány announces the first American tour of Diaghilev's troupe, in 1916. Diaghilev's name, variously spelled in transliterations, dominates many dance-memorabilia collections.

118 / DANCE MEMORABILIA

A bronze figurine (above) of Isadora Duncan performing her own "La Marseillaise" presents her barefooted, wearing Greek-inspired robes that she favored.

Hand-painted leather cigar cases of the mid-19th Century (above) picture Marie Taglioni dancing the title role of "La Sylphide," first staged in 1832.

Galina Ulanova, celebrated ballerina of the Soviet Union, is depicted on a gold-painted plaster plaque (above), made in the 1940s.

Unusual plywood cutouts (right), displaying pictures of Adolf Bolm (in three ballets) and Vera Nemtchinova, were made in England during the 1920s. They were meant to decorate mantels or whatnot shelves.

Anna Pavlova, Alexandra Danilova, Adolf Bolm and a number of other dancers of renown—appeared in the East and as far west as St. Paul. I once discovered a program for an 1857 Cecchetti performance in one of a dozen or so cartons of paper memorabilia I bought at a special sale in Boston. Such paper memorabilia—programs, pictures, autographs and window cards (posters 18 by 24 inches used for display in store windows)—are the easiest to locate.

Obviously, older material is as a rule more valuable, but this is not always the case. An old program is not automatically of great value unless it records a landmark event, such as the first performance of a new work that has since become a standard part of the repertoire of important companies, or the debut of a dancer who has since become a star. A good example of a notable debut is the first appearance of the fabled Nijinsky in the United States in 1916. Similarly, the program for the first stage appearance of Rudolf Nureyev in the United States after he left the Soviet Union (in *Don Quixote* at the Brooklyn Academy of Music in 1962) is one to find and keep. So is the program for the premiere of *Jewels*, which was choreographed by George Balanchine at the New York State Theater in 1967.

Present-day material—which, if you are discriminating, can become valuable—is of course easy to come by. If you ask the manager of a theater for dance programs that will be discarded after a troupe has finished its engagement, he often will give them to you. Autographs and photographs of contemporary leading dancers can be had for the asking by those who persevere. If you write a letter with requests for information (How old were you when you began to study dance? Which are your favorite ballets?) you may be rewarded with a personal, and valuable, reply. To obtain the signatures of the most famous artists you practically always must go to dealers. An autograph of Nijinsky or Pavlova would be quite expensive; the signatures of living dancers, even the most notable ones such as Nureyev, Baryshnikov and Makarova, far, far less.

Even more valuable and more difficult to find are the personal items of dancers, such as their shoes. Ballerinas usually wear toe-dancing shoes for only one show, and a request after the performance might conceivably be answered with the gift of a shoe ready to be discarded. Costumes, and the artist's sketches for costumes and sets, are also rare.

Some of the more desirable sketches are those that were commissioned by Diaghilev because he somehow managed to wangle set and costume designs from a number of leading names in the world of art. Among them were Georges Braque, Giorgio de Chirico, Pavel Tchelitchev and even Pablo Picasso. Prices of the work done for Diaghilev by these artists frequently go into the thousands of dollars. However, the ballet-inspired work of these artists generally goes for a price lower than that of their other creations because most collectors of art consider them to be less important works. Among artists' names that are associated with other ballet companies or with particular choreographers are Léon Bakst, Alexandre Benois, Marie Laurençin, Leonor Fini and Christian Bérard.

I have made a number of memorable discoveries of artworks, books and other items in out-of-the-way bookshops and in charity outlets. In a charity store not too long ago I happened to spot a copy of the *Complete Book of Ballets*, written by the late Cyril W. Beaumont, a noted English ballet critic whose books are now very difficult to locate. This particular one, which has been long out of print, was tagged "5¢."

Occasionally, ordinary antique dealers and secondhand shops will have mementos of American dancers, stars such as Isadora Duncan and Ruth St. Denis, who were the precursors in the early 1920s of modern dance. These performers achieved as much publicity for the flamboyance of their personal styles as they did for their innovations in dance. I once located as the result of a tip an enormous oil painting, 9 feet tall, of a woman in a diaphanous, Oriental costume. The portrayal was that of one of the stage manifestations of the modern dancer Ruth St. Denis.

Sheet music is a common item in secondhand stores, and it frequently provides dance memorabilia that is worth having. You can still come across sheet music of the old popular songs. Some of it goes back far enough to provide fascinating glimpses of 19th Century dance in America. Splendid illustrations of tap dancing and the cakewalk are to be seen on many of the covers of the sheet music of the period.

But for the most sought-after items, such as the dance programs that were illustrated by Picasso *(page 116)*, you have to go to dealers—a few, such as the Norman Crider Gallery and the Dance Mart of New York City, specialize in dance memorabilia. Learning the art of bargaining with dealers is useful, for once in a while they will accept an extra copy of a collectible you have and discount the price on a new purchase.

Be cautious of throwing away your memorabilia, however; I once acquired a dance-shoe manufacturer's advertising piece that came in the form of a comic-book biography of the great Pavlova—a merchandiser's inspiration that at that time seemed to me in questionable taste. I held onto it, however, and today I have found, to my surprise, that my comic-book Pavlova has become a valuable collectible.

For related material, see the article on Autographs in a separate volume of this encyclopedia.

120 / DANCE MEMORABILIA

Beside a headdress that was worn by Tamara Karsavina in the title role of "Firebird" in 1910 is a rare picture postcard of this noted Russian ballerina.

Two unusually large sketches for "Le Coq d'Or"—a ballet-opera with one cast to dance and one to sing—are 3 feet tall. They are preliminary drawings of the Queen of Shemakhan (left) and the Astrologer made by Natalia Gontcharova, who designed the settings and costumes for the 1914 European premiere at the Paris Opera. Her signature makes them a collector's prize.

The author's collection includes a frayed toe slipper (above) that was worn around 1911 by Pavlova, one of the now-legendary names of the early 20th Century.

At right are papier-mâché props representing jurors from "Hear Ye, Hear Ye!" This 1934 ballet about a jury trial was choreographed by Ruth Page to music by Aaron Copland.

DANCE MEMORABILIA / 121

French artist Marie Laurençin drew these sketches in watercolor for "Les Biches," a ballet choreographed to the music of fellow countryman Francis Poulenc and produced by Diaghilev in the 1920s. The handwritten sheets are from Laurençin's correspondence on the costumes.

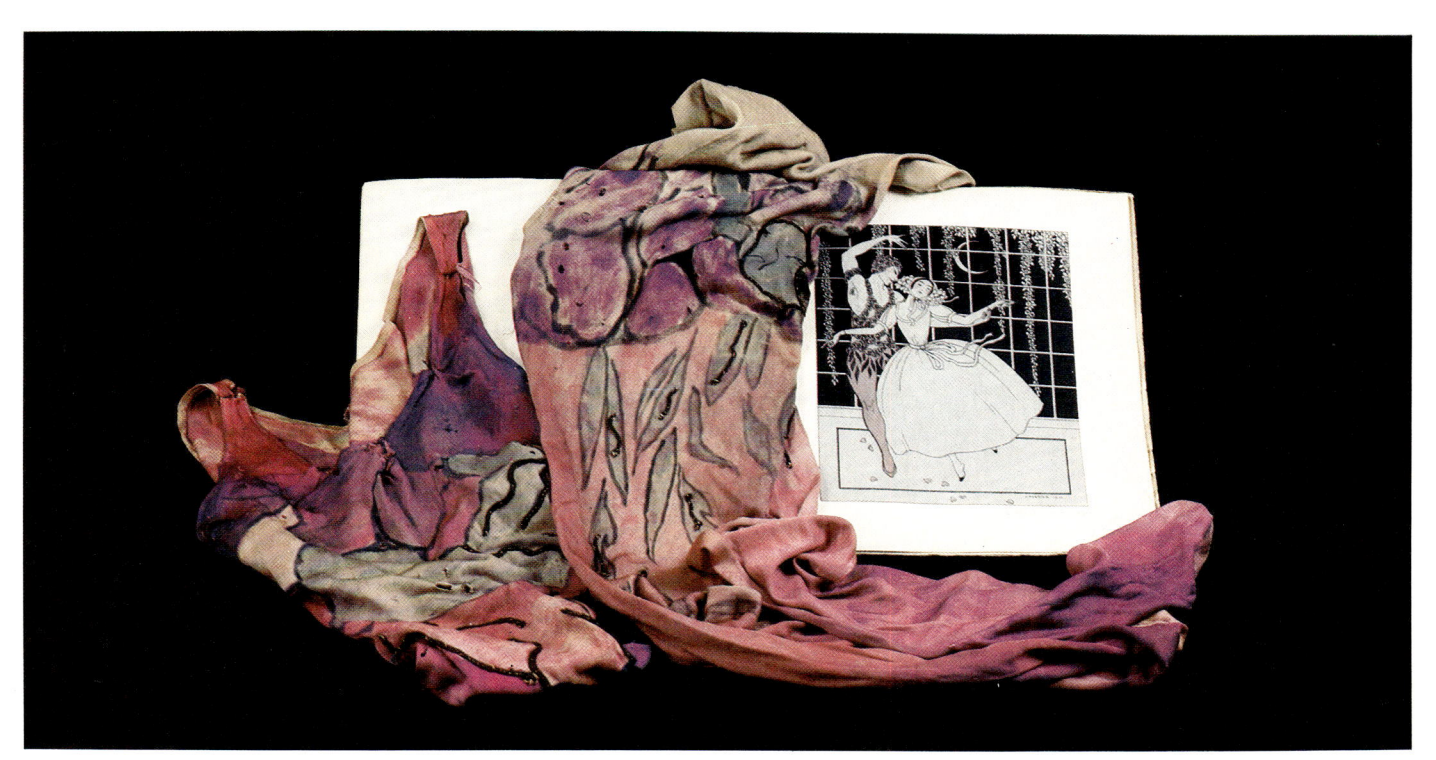

The clothing remnant above is from the costume worn by the fabled Nijinsky in Fokine's "Le Spectre de la Rose." Léon Bakst, a designer for opera and ballet, designed the costume and also drew the sketch next to it, of Tamara Karsavina, Nijinsky's partner.

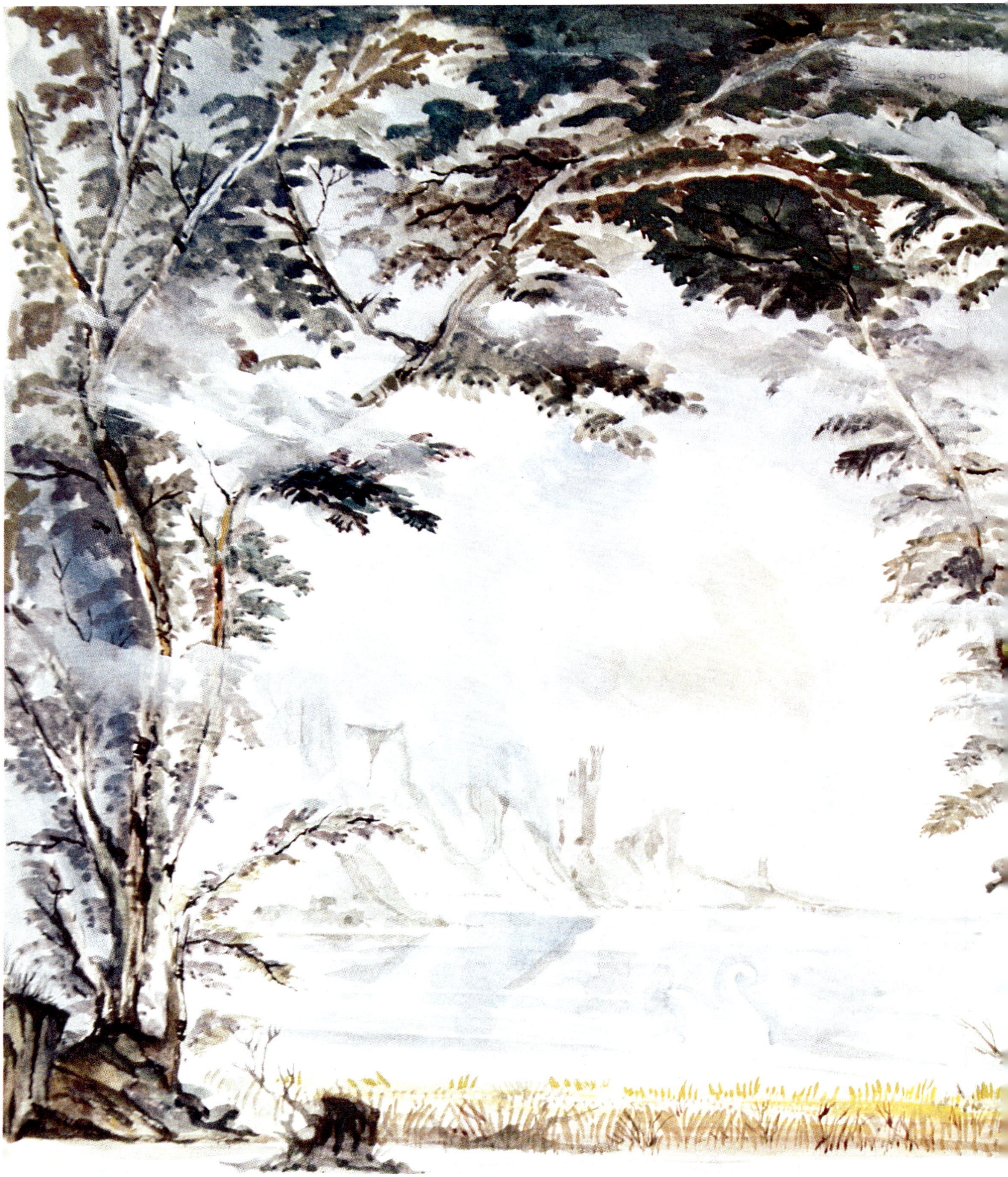

DANCE MEMORABILIA / 123

Costume sketches for "Swan Lake" by Russian designer Alexandre Benois were made for a planned 1945 production, never staged.

Theatrical designer Oliver Smith painted this watercolor (left) of a set that he created for the American Ballet Theatre's 1967 production of Act II of "Swan Lake."

124 / DANCE MEMORABILIA

Doris Humphrey, a pioneer of modern American dance, is flanked by two members of her company on a 1921 vaudeville tour. She later recalled in her autobiography that the backdrop was a velvet cyclorama decorated with rather gaudy bouquets.

This close-up of Pavlova is a still from "The Dumb Girl of Portici," a 1915 American film in which the ballerina played a dramatic role.

Ruth St. Denis strikes a precisely calculated pose for "Street Nautch," one of her many interpretations of traditional Indian dances, done in the early 1920s.

A rare photo of George Balanchine shows him in costume for "Triumph of Neptune," staged by Ballet Russe in 1928.

In a signed 1917 picture, modern-dance pioneers Ted Shawn and Ruth St. Denis strike a pose from "Dance of Rebirth," a work recalling ancient Egyptian hieroglyphs. Partners onstage, they were married and ran a dance school, Denishawn, in Los Angeles.

Dancing for the Devil of It

Many collectors seek mementos of social dancing—dancing for the fun of it at a formal ball, a prom in a college gymnasium, between drinks in a nightclub, or in a living room with the rug rolled up. The invitations (many of them elaborately printed), "cards" (often embossed and decorated with tassels) to record dances promised to partners, and books detailing codes of ballroom etiquette are prized for their nostalgia as well as for their value as social history.

But some of the more interesting social-dancing memorabilia are the antidance publications of the 19th Century denouncing any kind of dancing as satanic immorality. Proclaimed one of the preachments: "The dancing hall is the nursery of the divorce court, the training ship of prostitution, the graduating school of infamy."

An antidance booklet of about 1900 (left) defined the ballroom as "the greatest feeder of the brothel."

Dance cards—where a young lady of the mid-1800s listed her partners—are surrounded by invitations and dance instruction manuals.

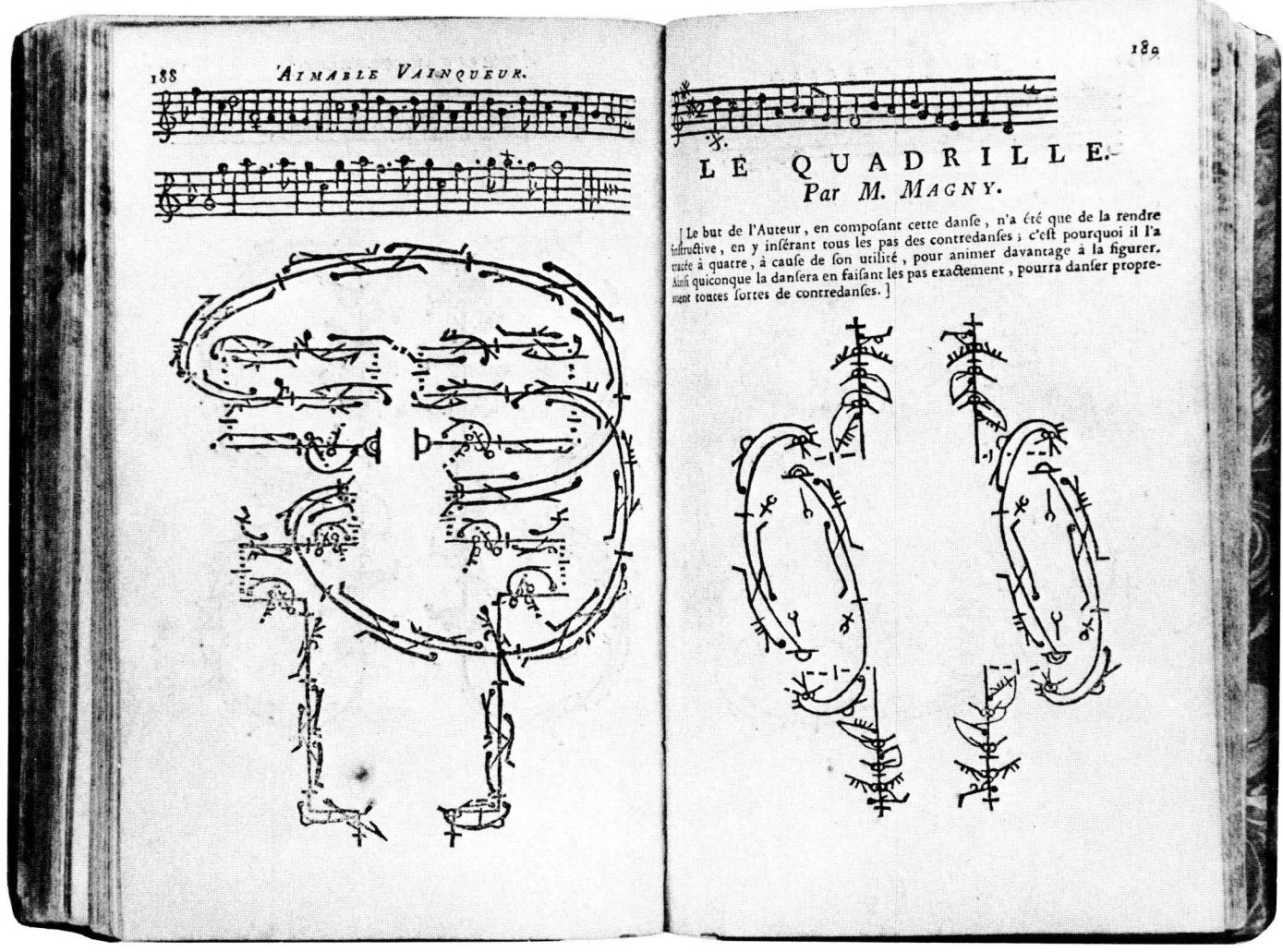

Among many systems for recording choreography are these, from Pierre Magny's 1765 "Les Principes de Choreographie." At left is a notation for part of a ballet called the "Aimable Vainqueur," done in the Louis Pécour system; at right are Magny's own directions for the quadrille.

MUSEUMS AND LIBRARIES
Birmingham Public Library
Birmingham, Alabama 35203

Hobilitzelle Theatre Arts Library
University of Texas
Austin, Texas 78712

Houghton Library Theatre Collection
Harvard University
Cambridge, Massachusetts 02138

New York Public Library and
Museum of the Performing Arts at
Lincoln Center
New York, New York 10023

University Archives
University of Illinois Library
Urbana, Illinois 61801

BOOKS
Beaumont, Cyril W., *Complete Book of Ballets.* Grosset & Dunlap Publishers, 1938.

Bland, Alexander, *A History of Ballet and Dance in the Western World.* Barrie & Jenkins, 1976.

Chujoy, Anatole, and P. W. Manchester, eds., *The Dance Encyclopedia.* Simon & Schuster, 1967.

Kirstein, Lincoln, *Dance, a Short History of Classic Theatrical Dancing.* Dance Horizons, Inc., 1969.

Spencer, Charles, *The World of Serge Diaghilev.* Henry Regnery Company, 1974.

Terry, Walter, *Ballet Guide.* Popular Library, 1977.

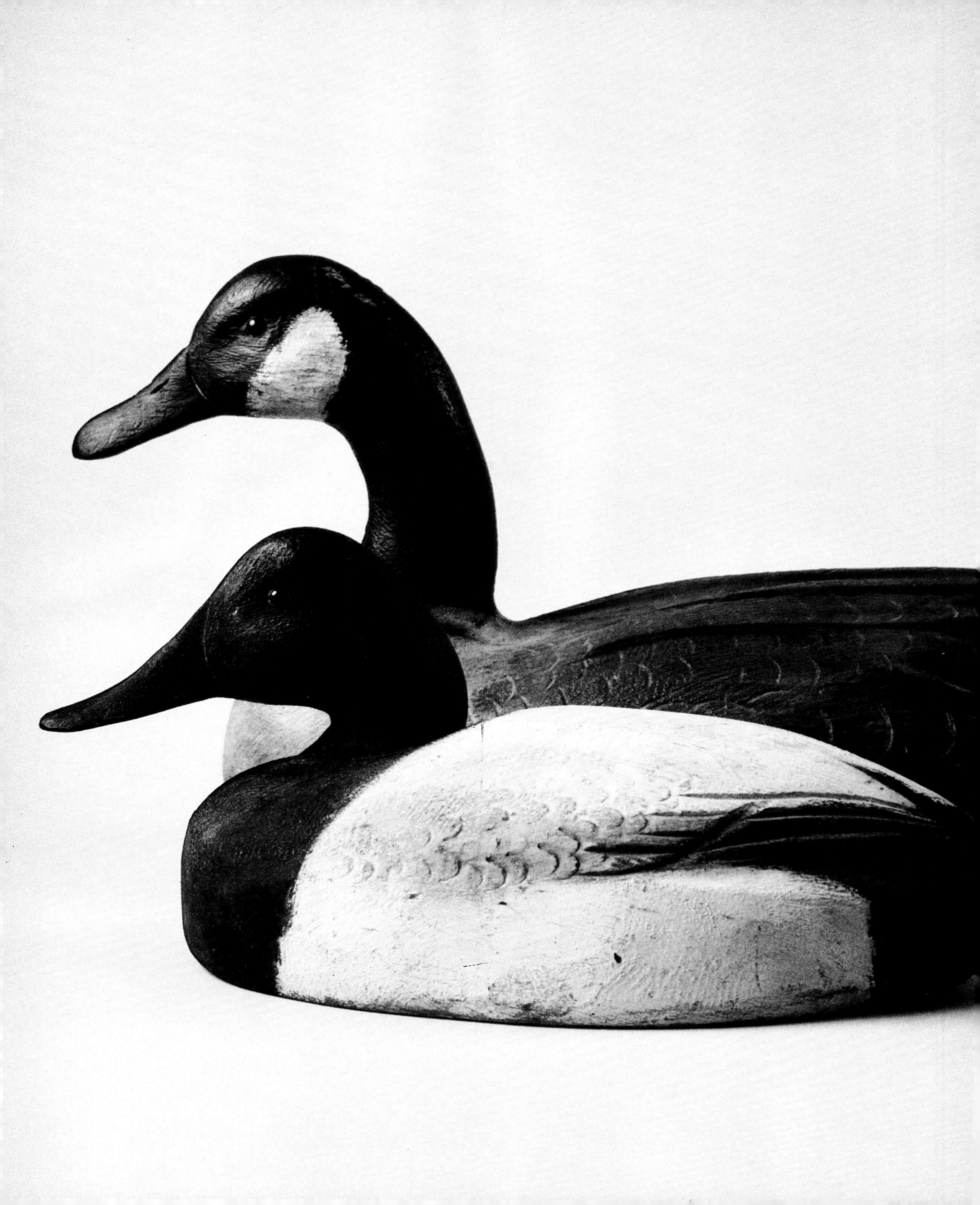

Decoys
Lures for Birds— and Collectors

There is an old joke among decoy collectors that humans are more easily lured by decoys than birds are. Collectors have foraged about in bays and along seashores, inside old boathouses and under abandoned docks, hoping to discover a decoy a hunter may have lost or discarded. What turns up under the boathouse floor—or more frequently these days, on the auction block at a price that may reach into the thousands of dollars—ranges from a 4-foot Canada goose that once bobbed in rough waters off New England to a tiny teal, just a few inches long, that came from California. Some decoys are nothing more than crudely

Gene and Linda Kangas began collecting decoys in 1970. They have written many articles on decoys, and worked on a TV program about folk art. Mr. Kangas teaches sculpture at Cleveland State University.

rendered silhouettes, while others are finely carved, painstakingly painted likenesses. A few originated in the shops of well-known carvers, but many are the work of anonymous craftsmen. The craft is both very old and uniquely American, for the inventors of the artificial decoy were North American Indians *(page 130)*.

Although decoys have been made in North America for centuries, the ones collectors prize are those produced since the mid-1800s. In the 19th Century, demand for meat made large-scale goose and duck hunting profitable. Professional "market gunners" each used as many as 600 decoys, which they set out in water or on land to tempt birds on their migratory flights to come within shooting distance. During these migrations enormous flocks journeyed back and forth between South America and Canada along four major flyways—the Atlantic Coast, the Mississippi Valley, the Pacific Coast and a broad route, called Central, between the Mississippi and the Rockies. Types of species, as well as hunting techniques, varied from flyway to flyway, and decoys are

These duck and goose decoys are relatively modern but are nonetheless prized for their beauty. They were made in the 1940s or 1950s by Benjamin Schmidt, a noted Michigan carver, who cut the wood so that the feathers seem to stand away from the body.

An Indian Invention

A startlingly realistic decoy made by Indians around 1000 A.D. consists of bundled bulrushes and feathers.

Wild fowl have been hunted by men all over the world since prehistoric times, but American Indians were apparently the first to use artificial decoys to lure birds to the hunter's grasp. The example above, made of reeds and feathers, is one of 11 found by archeologists in Lovelock Cave, Nevada, in 1924. Made around the 10th Century, they are the earliest specimens known. Paiute Indians in the Southwest and others still make decoys this way. Another method is simply to stuff skins of birds for lures, a practice still in use but one of great age. In a letter in 1687, French Baron de Lahontan wrote of Indians using "the skins of Geese, Bustards, and Ducks, dry'd and stuff'd with Hay."

often classified according to the flyway for which they were designed. Most decoys that are collected were used along the Atlantic and Mississippi flyways, where the hunting was most intense.

Overzealous shooting led to the extinction of a number of species, and by the 1920s commercial bird hunting had been outlawed and sport shooting regulated. Many carvers gave up making decoys and turned instead to making ornamental wood sculptures of game birds. Collectors generally pass these by in favor of the old working decoys, those that were actually used by a hunter. However, a few carvers continued to produce working decoys for amateur sportsmen, and some of the most sought-after decoys were made as late as the 1940s and 1950s by such master carvers as Charles "Shang" Wheeler of Connecticut, Lem and Steve Ward of Maryland, Elmer Crowell of Cape Cod, Mark Whipple of Louisiana and Luigi Andreuccetti of California.

Identifying decoys by these carvers is not always simple. Crowell helpfully stamped his name on the base of his work, but the products of the others have to be recognized by appearance. The Wards, for example, favored duck decoys whose heads were turned to one side. Wheeler's ducks were hollow and ballasted with oval weights to make them ride with their breasts above water. The best place to look for decoys is in the areas where the carvers lived and worked.

Although most collectors specialize, in most cases they do so not by the date of the decoys' origin, but by the flyway where they were used, by the species of bird that are represented or by makers. Altogether, carvers produced decoys for 30 or so different species of duck and goose. Some decoys, such as the ruddy duck and shoveler, are hard to find. Others, such as the canvasback, are common. Mallard decoys are most often encountered along the Mississippi flyway. Old-squaw decoys are vir-

A decoy made between 1860 and 1880 for the Atlantic flyway by John Blair, a Philadelphia portrait painter, reflects his knowledge of paint—after many years of use it is still in nearly perfect condition.

John Heisler, a hunting guide, carved this resting black duck around 1910. It is oversized but hollow to keep its weight low. Heisler worked the Delaware River area of the Atlantic flyway.

tually unknown there but are found in the northern segment of the Atlantic flyway.

For any kind of bird, there are two main types of decoy. One floats; the other is the "stick-up"—a full-sized decoy mounted on a stake. A variant of the stick-up is the silhouette, called a shadow, profile or flatty. Most stick-ups are for shore birds, most floating decoys for ducks and geese.

Regional differences help the collector identify origin. Along the Mississippi flyway, profile stick-ups of ducks and geese are common because a type of hunting called pit shooting was practiced there. The hunter dug a pit in a field and set out decoys around the pit. Such profiles are seldom seen elsewhere, since dry-land pit shooting was a Mississippi specialty.

A specialty of the Atlantic flyway is oversized goose decoys made of slats *(page 138)* to save weight. Their unusual size was intended to draw birds from far off. Slat goose bodies are crudely shaped, but some necks and heads, especially those carved by Elmer Crowell and Joseph Lincoln, are finely crafted.

Floating decoys of the Mississippi flyway are similar to those used in New Jersey and Connecticut because the design was passed along, with certain modifications, from carver to carver. The original decoys were designed for New Jersey's Barnegat Bay, where shallow-draft boats were used, and decoys had to be hollow and lightweight to keep from overloading the craft. A Connecticut carver of hollow decoys, Albert Laing, worked out a modification of the design that would keep his birds afloat in the slush ice of the Housatonic River. Benjamin Holmes, a carver who followed Laing's design, exhibited some of his own decoys at the Centennial Exhibition in Philadelphia in 1876, where there they were viewed by Robert Elliston, a carver from Illinois. Elliston admired the hollow design, copied it, and was in turn emulated by other Midwestern carvers.

One Atlantic flyway decoy not seen elsewhere is the wing duck. Usually designed to look like the ducks known as canvasbacks or redheads, the wing decoys were made of cast iron. They did their decoy duty while acting as weights on floating "batteries"—small, one-man boats with wooden "wings" extending out from the hull on all sides. The wing ducks, which weighed as much as 50 pounds each, were placed on the wings to keep the battery riding low in the water, and thus less likely to be noticed. These weighty decoys can still be found in areas around old docks on Long Island, Chesapeake Bay, the Back Bay areas of Virginia, and along the coast of North Carolina.

The Atlantic flyway is also the best place to look for stick-up decoys of shore birds such as curlews, plovers and yellowlegs *(pages 132-133)*. The best-made and now most sought-after are from Cape Cod.

In the heyday of market gunning, demand for decoys led to the production of factory-made decoys. The most sought-after are those produced by the Harvey A. Stevens Company of Weedsport, New York, which stenciled or burned its name on its products, and two Detroit firms, Mason Decoy Factory and Jasper N. Dodge Company, both of which made decoys distinguished by swirling, textured paint.

On both factory- and hand-made decoys, the condition of the paint is one of the more reliable guides to age and value. The old decoys used by market gunners were given a new coat of paint every year or so, and many layers of cracked and checked paint therefore suggest great age. The paint of Midwestern decoys, which were used in fresh water, is usually in better condition than that of Atlantic flyway decoys, which were subjected to the harsher environment of salt water.

A well-preserved paint job adds greatly to desirability, but collectors rarely repaint a decoy; the original paint, even if it is scratched or faded, is considered the most valuable. To find out if the paint on a decoy has been touched up, you can examine it with ultraviolet light, sometimes called black light, from a lamp available at most hobby stores. In a darkened room, the black light will make the decoy glow, or fluoresce. A spot of new paint, which might reveal a repair that would lessen value, will fluoresce more brightly than old.

Scratches and nicks are an indication of use, but if you notice that a surface has been heavily scratched, or if there is evidence of wood putty, particularly where the head and body come together, you may have come across an example of a new head married to an old body that had lost its own. In a case of this sort, an X-ray of the decoy may reveal the presence of a new nail or hidden putty *(box, page 137)*. Such repairs are common and they may decrease value, depending on how recently they were made.

You may find a name or date stamped on the decoy. Although carvers seldom signed their work, the stamp may help in identification. Generally, a name stamped on a decoy is the owner's name, not the maker's, but this fact itself can help in tracing a decoy's history.

An excellent source of information is a local hunter or guide, preferably one with a long memory. The late William J. Mackey Jr., an eminent collector, visited an old hunter in Maryland to show him an unusual balsa shorebird decoy that Mackey believed was the work of a master carver named Ira Hudson. The hunter took a quick look. "Yes," he said at once, "I recollect the day Ira and I dragged that log out of the surf on Assateague Island. He made that very bird from it in 1916."

For related material, see the articles on Folk Art and Weather Vanes in separate volumes of this encyclopedia.

Shore birds of many species were lured by "stick-ups" set in the ground on the edge of the water where they sought their food. Here, from left to right, are six that were used along the Atlantic flyway: a 1910 curlew from North Carolina, an 1890 yellowlegs from New England, a yellowlegs made by New Jersey artist Joel Barkelow around 1870, an 1890 snipe from North Carolina, a New Jersey black-breasted plover done around 1900 and a silhouette, probably intended to look like a curlew, that was made in North Carolina.

Decoys for Fish

Native Americans crafted decoys to capture fish as well as fowl; some spear fishermen among the Eskimos still produced decoys in the late 20th Century, using them to lure fish toward holes cut in the ice. The art has flourished elsewhere in America—notably in Minnesota, Wisconsin, Michigan, New York and New England—but some states now restrict or ban freshwater spear fishing through ice.

Fish decoys may be deployed four or more on one line. They are carved from bone or wood and weighted with lead for ballast. After the decoy rig is suspended in the water, the hunter plays the line with his fingers in an attempt to simulate the swimming of live fish.

Fish decoys are generally small, 6 to 12 inches, but imitation fish 3 feet or more in length have been made, doubling as measuring sticks to gauge the legality of a catch.

The ability of a spear fisherman to make the decoys' swimming action realistic is sometimes enhanced by the addition to the bodies of fins and tails of leather, wood or metal. Nailed into slots in the body of the decoy, the artificial fins cause it to circle when the tether line is pulled.

Painted fish decoys are made to be true to life, with light bellies and dark backs, although sequins and glitter are occasionally added to make the decoys more visible in dark waters.

For some, a mesh screen has been used to stencil a crosshatch pattern suggesting scales.

Fish decoys make their way to auction sales of bird decoys, and the best place to look is in the regions where ice fishing was most popular. The value of a fish decoy rises with its realism. Primitive, stylized decoys were selling for less than $10 in the 1970s. Realistic paint, fins, tails and glass eyes increase the value—to as much as 10 or 20 times that of the simplest decoy.

Two bass decoys for Midwestern ice fishing were carved by Hans Jenner Sr. around 1930.

A black duck with wings of tin, designed to be used on the Mississippi flyway before 1900, was set on a stick in shallow water. The duck imitates a live bird heading into the wind and preparing to make a landing.

Two decoys, in a style first popularized in Connecticut, imitate a goldeneye hen (in front) and a redhead. Thomas Chambers of Michigan did the redhead; the goldeneye was probably done by Nate Quillen of Toronto.

These canvasbacks are long-necked examples very rare in the Michigan area of the Mississippi flyway. They are the work of Edward "One-Arm" Kellie, a handicapped railroadman of Michigan.

A canvasback duck carved in Michigan for the Mississippi flyway has a special feature: a "pistol-grip" head and neck, used as a handle when the hunter threw the decoy out into the water.

This pair of humpbacked bluebill duck decoys is from Wisconsin. They were produced by a carver named John Roth of Wisconsin and are relatively recent, dating from the 1930s.

136 / DECOYS

A preening mallard by Mitchell LaFrance, a prominent Louisiana carver of this century, exemplifies his expertise in both woodwork and painting. Decoys made in the South tended to stay close to home and are rare in collections assembled elsewhere in the country.

This elegant pintail decoy was produced sometime before the Second World War by Mark Whipple of Louisiana; the pintail species is extensively hunted in that state. The long tail alone accounts for about one quarter of the duck's length.

X-Ray Evaluation

To detect recent repairs that may affect the value of a decoy, you can have it X-rayed—a local medical laboratory will do the job if you explain what you are about. The example at left indicates that this redhead is exactly the way Thomas Chambers made it in 1890. If the X-ray had shown a nail in the neck covered with putty—which would appear as a light spot or line—a repair probably had been made. The neck, head and bill are the areas that are most frequently repaired.

An X-ray of a decoy reveals the neck joint—with no telltale light areas indicating repairs.

Not all decoys are carved. The black duck in the foreground, its head bent in an exaggerated feeding position, was constructed around 1900 of stuffed canvas. The Illinois River goose was made of laminated wooden planks in the 1930s.

138 / DECOYS

The size of decoys varies greatly. The oversized goose, built of wooden slats and log sections, is a "loomer." Set with others in the water, it and its mates could be spotted from far off, attracting distant flocks to the hunters. The tiny decoys are for West Coast teal.

Folk carvers often adapted natural materials in ingenious ways. The bodies of these rustic brant geese decoys are carved California redwood, while the heads are root sections left largely untouched. Both of these "root-head" specimens from the Pacific flyway date from about 1910.

The wily crow has been lured into shooting range by fake crows and owls like these. Crows hate owls so much that they will flock to harass one, oblivious to a hunter. The owl above is wooden; stuffed ones, sometimes rigged to flap their wings, have also been used.

MUSEUMS
Cleveland Museum of Natural History
Cleveland, Ohio 44106

Museum of American Folk Art
New York, New York 10019

Shelburne Museum
Shelburne, Vermont 05482

COLLECTORS ORGANIZATIONS
Long Island Decoy Collectors Association
139 Prospect Street
Babylon, New York 11702

Midwest Decoy Collectors Association
1400 South 58th Street
Lincoln, Nebraska 68506

PERIODICALS
Decoy Collector's Guide, Harold D. Sorenson, 312 Franklin Street, Burlington, Iowa 52601

Decoy World, M. Clark Reed Jr., 115 South Main Street, Trappe, Maryland 21613

North American Decoys, Bryan Cheever, P.O. Box 246, Spanish Fork, Utah 84660

BOOKS
Barber, Joel, *Wild Fowl Decoys.* Dover Publications, Inc., 1954.

Bellrose, Frank, *Ducks, Geese & Swans of North America.* Stackpole Books, 1976.

Burk, Bruce, *Game Bird Carving.* Winchester Press, 1972.

Earnest, Adele, *The Art of the Decoy: American Bird Carvings.* Bramhall House, 1965.

Elman, Robert, *The Atlantic Flyway.* Winchester Press, 1972.

Johnsgard, Paul A., *The Bird Decoy.* University of Nebraska Press, 1976.

Mackey, William J., Jr., *American Bird Decoys.* E. P. Dutton & Company, Inc., 1965.

Richardson, R. H., *Chesapeake Bay Decoys.* Tidewater Publishers, 1973.

Rue, Leonard Lee, III, *Game Birds of North America.* Harper and Row, 1973.

Starr, George Ross, Jr., *Decoys of the Atlantic Flyway.* Winchester Press, 1974.

Webster, David S., and William Kehoe, *Decoys at Shelburne Museum.* Hobby House, 1961.

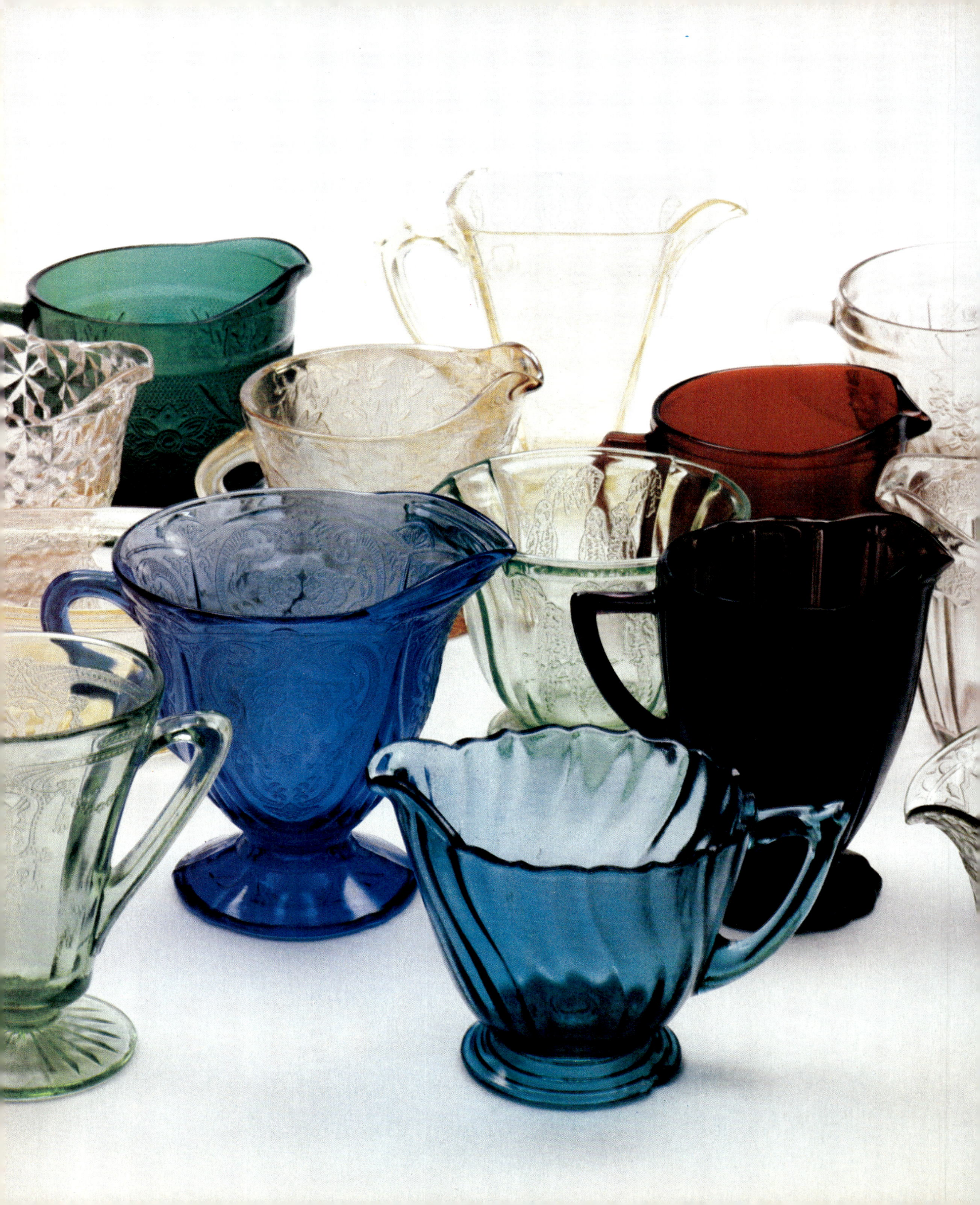

Depression Glass
Cheery Reminders of Grim Days

There was a time when you could get glassware like the creamers at left for nothing. More than that, getting it provided an excuse to go to the movies during the Depression. As the doorman took your ticket on "dish night," he gave you a dish. Oldtimers can recall the startling sound of dishes crashing at the end of the show as people stood up to leave and forgot the fragile giveaways on their laps. But if you remembered, and you went to the movies every week on dish night, you acquired free a set of dishes made of what is now called Depression glass.

Of course, Depression glass was also sold through mail-order houses and five-and-ten-cent stores, some

---

Debra Terceira, manager of an insurance office, and Robert Abbate, an accountant, both of Long Island, New York, began collecting Depression glass together in 1971, before their marriage.

---

pieces costing no more than three cents each. Over a generation these wares became collectibles, partly out of nostalgia, partly because of their cheery colors. More than 100 collectors clubs sprang up, and big, regularly scheduled shows were put on. A magazine on the subject tripled its circulation in less than a decade.

Nevertheless, dealers' prices for Depression glass remained well below those for fine antiques. Almost any piece could be had for less than $20 in the late 1970s, and many were less than five dollars. And much Depression glass still is free—in attics and cellars, where broken sets were consigned as families replaced them with better tableware. Rummaging in an attic, buying at garage sales, you can find a few unmatched plates and cups here, a bowl there and a pitcher elsewhere. Eventually you will find that your pieces begin to match.

The everyday wares that attract such interest are cheap, machine-molded pieces produced from the mid-1920s into the 1940s. Most of them were made by such companies as: Federal Glass Company of Columbus, Ohio; Hazel Atlas Glass Company of Clarksville, West Virginia; Hocking Glass Company of Lancaster, Ohio; Indiana Glass Company of Dunkirk, Indiana; Jeannette Glass Company of Jeannette, Pennsylvania; and Macbeth-Evans Glass Company of Charleroi, Pennsylvania. Some collectors look for all American glass of that period, including higher-quality products, as well as post-1950 reissues made in the old molds.

Depression glass came in more than 25 colors—transparent, translucent or opaque—and in more than 95 patterns. Pattern, color and the intended purpose of a piece all affect value. Several desirable patterns are illustrated in the accompanying photographs. Collectors identify many of the colors by the manufacturers' trade names: The most common transparent colors are pastel pinks, greens and ambers such as Nu-Rose, Springtime Green and Golden Glow. Fewer pieces are found in light blue, deep Ritz Blue and deep ruby red. Smoke—bluish gray with a black stripe—is very rare. Colorless transparent pieces, referred to as crystal, are fairly common. Among the opaque colors are Delfite Blue and Jadite. Monax resembles milk glass, while Cremax, a creamy beige, is both a color and a pattern name. The color's effect on price is shown by the American Sweetheart pattern on page 147. In Smoke, a 10-inch dinner plate is worth nearly four times its value in Monax.

Shape can be as important as color in determining value. Saucers were the most common pieces and are the least expensive. Dinner plates are costlier; sugar-and-cream and salt-and-pepper sets, both collectors' favorites, are more expensive still. Most difficult to find unchipped and uncracked is a round butter dish with a domed cover. Because the dish was continually in and out of the refrigerator, many tops were broken.

Kitchenware of all kinds is a collecting specialty. Some collectors even limit themselves to juicers, produced in hundreds of slightly different versions.

Certain pieces are bargains even at high prices. A covered butter dish or any sizable piece with a cover or a foot is such a find. So is a sandwich server—a plate with a handle in its center. In the Cameo pattern on page 148, and in green, it could bring hundreds of dollars.

For related material, see the article on Carnival Glass in another volume of this encyclopedia.

These 14 cream pitchers indicate the range of colors and patterns in the inexpensive ware called Depression glass. Among the more desirable examples are the ultramarine Swirl in the foreground, the blue Royal Lace just behind it to the left and the amethyst Newport to the right.

142 / DEPRESSION GLASS

The serving bowl at right, of the type called a handled berry bowl, is scarce because its Doric and Pansy pattern was made for only two years, 1937 and 1938.

The Iris pattern of the cream pitcher and butter dish above was introduced in 1928, but these pieces are more recent—their iridescent color was not used until 1950. Most glassware produced in the 1920s and '30s by the maker, Jeannette Glass Company, was clear, pink or green.

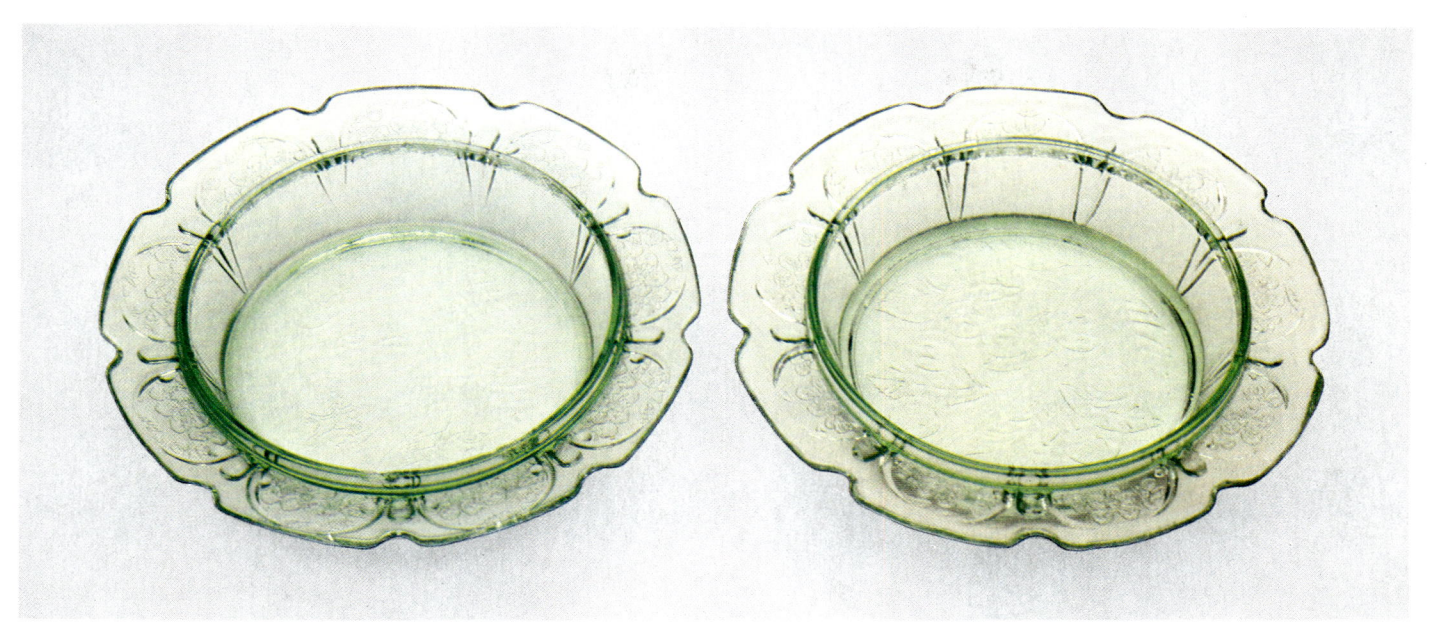

Both of these butter dishes, shown without their covers, are in the widely collected Cherry Blossom pattern, but only the one at left was produced in the 1930s. The other, made in the 1970s, is recognizable as a copy because the pattern stops short of the rim.

This child's set—cup and saucer, dinner plate, creamer and sugar bowl—in the Cherry Blossom pattern is about one third the size of regular tableware. Finding such a set in the cardboard box in which it originally was sold adds to its value.

144 / DEPRESSION GLASS

A detail of a lunch plate (right) reveals the stylized floral design of the popular Florentine II pattern. The same pattern decorates the serving set below; because it is complete with the original carrying tray, it is extremely rare.

The Royal Lace pattern was used by Hazel Atlas Glass Company for a variety of shapes. A detail of a platter is above. At left is a set of salt-and-pepper shakers, much sought after. Easier to find are (below, clockwise from the left) a creamed-soup bowl; a console, or centerpiece; a tumbler; and a cup and saucer. The most valuable pieces in this pattern are those in burgundy and in blue, a color added in 1936.

146 / DEPRESSION GLASS

The design on the covered refrigerator dish and batter bowl at right is a common one, but the bowl is unusual because it has a handle.

The Sharon pattern can readily be found in butter dishes and many other shapes—but not in the iced-tea glass at right. Few were made, and in excellent condition they are prizes.

The Dogwood pattern is seen here in pink, the color in which it is most commonly found. Dogwood, very popular with collectors, was made between 1928 and 1932 in a number of other colors: green, yellow, clear, milky white and a creamy white or beige.

This 11-inch American Sweetheart bowl is in possibly the most popular pattern made by the Macbeth-Evans Glass Company. The pattern was made in more colors than most glassware of the period: pink, red, Monax (milky white), Cremax (creamy white), blue, and black-trimmed Smoke.

148 / DEPRESSION GLASS

The butter dish at right is in Cameo, a prized pattern. The dish still has its cover; this adds to its value. In yellow, this piece is much rarer.

This pitcher and tumbler in the Sandwich pattern were made in the 1950s, and are therefore considered by some collectors to have been made too late to be true Depression glass.

Dinner plates in the Miss America pattern are readily found in pink and clear crystal. In blue and red the pattern, made from 1933 to 1936, is rare.

150 / DEPRESSION GLASS

Pastel swans are a specialized collectible in Depression glass, and matched pairs like this are rare. Made in various sizes, they were sometimes used as saltcellars.

Sets of toy dishes, like the one above, generally combined several opaque colors.

When Prohibition ended in 1933, whiskey sets of decanter and glasses became popular. This pattern is called Ring of Rings.

An unusual Depression glass find is a lamp with two ballerinas on the base. It was more expensive than other lamps, and few were sold.

An enamelware percolator with its original Depression-glass dome is fairly common, as are measuring cups, which many companies made.

COLLECTORS ORGANIZATIONS
Central Jersey Depression Glass Club
301 Maxson Avenue
Point Pleasant, New Jersey 08742

Del-Mar-Va Club
7420 Westlake Terrace
Bethesda, Maryland 20034

Depression Glass Grabbers of Historic Charleston
Route 6, Box 529H
Summerville, South Carolina 29483

Depression Glass of Northeast Florida
3243 Searchwood Street
Jacksonville, Florida 32211

Heart of America Glass Collectors
721 Cambridge Drive
Lee's Summit, Missouri 64063

International Depression Glass Club
4850 Broadway
Live Oak, California 95826

Long Island Depression Glass Society Ltd.
P.O. Box 119
West Sayville, New York 11796

Peach State Depression Glass Club
4329 South Main Street
Acworth, Georgia 30101

20-30-40 Society Chicagoland
811 W. Berkley Drive
Arlington Heights, Illinois 60004

PERIODICALS
Depression Glass Daze, P.O. Box 57, Otisville, Michigan 48463

National Depression Glass Journal, P.O. Box 268, Billings, Missouri 65610

BOOKS
Florence, Gene, *The Collectors Encyclopedia of Depression Glass,* 3rd ed., Collectors Books, 1977.

Klamkin, Marian, *The Collector's Guide to Depression Glass,* Hawthorn Books, Inc., 1973.

Weatherman, Hazel Marie:
Colored Glassware of the Depression Era, 2 vols. Glassbooks, Inc., Route 1, Box 357A, Ozark, Missouri 65721, 1974-1978.
Price Trends, 2 vols. Glassbooks, Inc., 1977-1978.

Detective Fiction
A Real Fascination with Imagined Crime

Collectors of detective fiction are afflicted with a particularly virulent form of what many of them cheerfully recognize as a disease. The world described in the books and magazines they collect so zealously is often more real to them than the one reported on in newspapers. They find it difficult to distinguish between people of historical authenticity and fictional characters. To many of them—to many of us, I should say—Sherlock Holmes is not the greatest fictional character ever invented; rather, he is the most famous person in history.

This affliction has led me to put together a hoard of more than 9,000 items, many of them discovered while

---

Otto Penzler is the author of "The Private Lives of Private Eyes," co-author of the "Encyclopedia of Mystery and Detection" and editor of "The Great Detectives."

---

on a trip spent scouring bookstores in England, Scotland and Ireland, looking for prizes from the 19th Century. It was toward the middle of that century that detective fiction made its first appearance in Western literature, although the Chinese had been writing similar works for centuries *(page 160)*. The father of the detective story is generally acknowledged to be the American writer Edgar Allan Poe, who in 1845 published *Tales,* a volume that included such stories as "The Murders in the Rue Morgue," "The Mystery of Marie Roget" and "The Purloined Letter."

One reader of Poe's stories was a young lawyer named Abraham Lincoln. He wrote a mystery story of his own, "The Trailor Murder Mystery," basing it on one of his cases. It was published in the April 15, 1846, issue of the *Whig,* a Quincy, Illinois, newspaper. A copy of Lincoln's tale would be a priceless treasure for any collector, but none is known to exist.

Authors more successful at fiction than Lincoln was developed Poe's prototypes into the mystery story as it now exists. *The Moonstone* by Wilkie Collins introduced in the person of its protagonist, Sergeant Cuff, the astute but unofficial-looking detective who set the style for many who followed.

But the greatest name in detective fiction is indisputably that of Sherlock Holmes, chronicled by Sir Arthur Conan Doyle in four novels and 56 short stories. Holmes first appeared in "A Study in Scarlet," a story in the 1887 issue of *Beeton's Christmas Annual*—a copy in fine condition was sold to the Metropolitan Library of Toronto in 1976 for $7,500. Holmesmania is not merely the basis of collectible No. 1 of detective fiction; it is really a separate world *(page 157)*.

Collectors have been tracking Poe, Collins, Conan Doyle and the other pioneers for so many years that a newcomer to the field can hope to do little but dream of finding early examples of their works. Most copies are in the secure custody of dealers and library exhibition cases. For a first edition of *The Moonstone,* identified by its purple binding and the date 1868 on the title page, $3,500 was paid in 1977. Poe's *Tales,* in fine condition, commanded $5,500 in the mid-1970s, but its value doubled, according to dealers' estimates, in the succeeding years. At much more reachable prices, however, splendid collectibles of detective fiction await the knowing— and assiduous—hunter.

A few years back, for example, I heard a rumor that there was a sizable collection of detective fiction for sale in the Midwest. After a year of asking around, I was finally able to confirm that a collector in Indiana had a large lot for sale. I got on the phone to him on a Friday, and the next morning caught a flight to Indiana in the company of another collector with whom I often hunt on a 50-50-split basis.

We were led to an attic, where we found some 11,000 volumes. After a full day and night of dusty work, we agreed to buy the entire lot. We packed four shopping bags with the best and flew home with them. The next week my colleague flew back and rented a truck to carry off the remainder of the haul—the biggest single purchase of my collecting career.

Most of the 11,000 were third- or fourth-rate, and soon were sold or traded. But each of us kept about 1,000 books. The haul yielded several prizes, including one, *The Curious Mr. Tarrant,* by C. Daly King, that is

A volume published in 1929 by the "first lady of crime," though labeled "A Detective Story," is in fact a series of parodies of detectives created by other writers, including Sherlock Holmes. This departure from the adventures of Agatha Christie's own Hercule Poirot adds value.

PARTNERS IN CRIME

A DETECTIVE STORY

BY

AGATHA CHRISTIE

Author of THE SEVEN DIALS MYSTERY

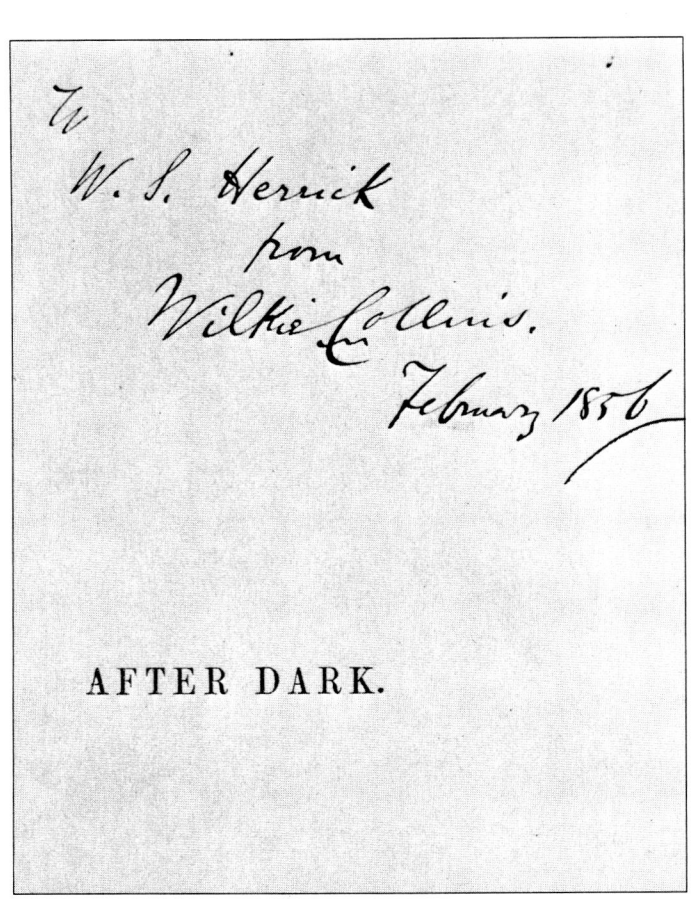

Wilkie Collins, author of "The Moonstone," the first detective novel to win a place in English literature, inscribed this copy of his earlier mystery, "After Dark," for a friend, W. S. Herrick, increasing its value.

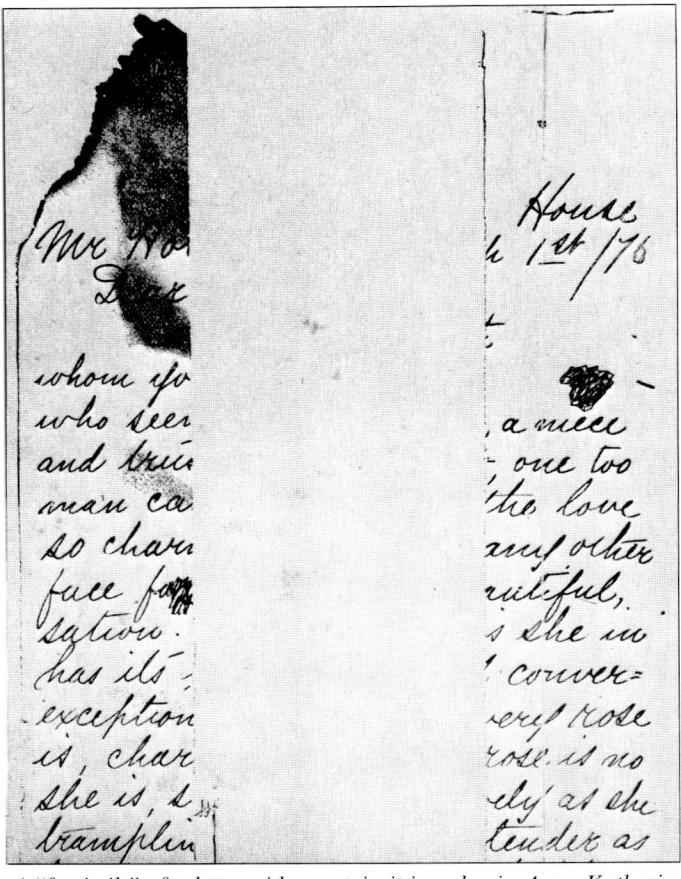

A "facsimile" of a letter with a gap in it is a clue in Anna Katharine Green's "The Leavenworth Case" of 1878. The letter was pasted into each copy and fell out of many, becoming a missing clue itself.

exceptionally rare in the original edition, published in England in 1935.

Perseverance also paid off for me in the Case of the Reluctant Bookseller. This gentleman had a shop in lower Manhattan that I visited frequently. I came to suspect that, in addition to the wares on display, a sizable detective-fiction collection existed in storage. I repeatedly asked the bookseller if I could have a look in his storeroom; he always refused. But then the bookseller lost his lease. I heard of his misfortune and promptly made a cold-blooded offer. I would help him with the gargantuan task of moving, for a price: I was to have first pick of any detective books I found. I must have moved thousands of books, but in the process I was able to carry off, wearily, several hundred finds, most of them for one dollar each. The best were some autographed "S. S. Van Dine."

In detective fiction of the 20th Century, S. S. Van Dine is a highly collectible name, one that belongs with a select coterie of writers who are esteemed for one or more reasons: because they invented a new style or a new school of mystery writing, or because they created fascinating characters, or constructed plots of remarkable ingenuity, or were able to evoke a fictional yet convincing world, or were simply writers of extraordinary skill and imagination.

Among the notable authors, to mention only a handful (and not in chronological order), are Ellery Queen, John P. Marquand, Mickey Spillane, Erle Stanley Gardner, Dashiell Hammett, James M. Cain, John Dickson Carr, Raymond Chandler, Cornell Woolrich, Graham Greene, Josephine Tey, Agatha Christie, Dorothy Sayers, Rex Stout, John Creasey and Ross Macdonald. First editions of their books, particularly of the early works that made their reputations, are ones to watch for.

When you are looking through stacks of old books for desirable titles, keep in mind the fact that a number of writers used pseudonyms. John Creasey, for example, adopted no fewer than 25 in the process of turning out nearly 600 books. My find in the Case of the Reluctant Bookseller, S. S. Van Dine, was a pseudonymous author, too, but a modest one who employed only that one pen name. Van Dine was actually an erudite art critic, Willard Huntington Wright, who introduced an equally

"The Diamond Coterie" was an early detective novel by a woman — Lawrence L. Lynch was really Emma Murdoch Van Deventer — as well as the first book published in the U.S. with a pictorial dust jacket.

erudite sleuth, Philo Vance, in 1926. That was in a book called *The Benson Murder Case.* The next year Van Dine produced *The Canary Murder Case,* which became a best-seller and was translated into seven languages. It was followed by 10 others.

Only first Philo Vance editions are considered collectibles. Those that appeared before 1930 — Scribner was the publisher — can be identified by simply comparing the date on the title page with the copyright date on the reverse side of that page: if the dates are the same, the book is most likely a first edition. Philo Vances that were published after 1930 are firsts if a capital A appears at the end of the copyright notice. Their value, depending on condition, is what might be called average — $25 or slightly more in the 1970s.

The first appearance of a sleuth makes a book a particularly desirable collectible, so look for these: *No Hero* by John P. Marquand (Mr. Moto, 1935), *Fer-de-Lance* by Rex Stout (Nero Wolfe, 1934), *The Case of the Velvet Claws* by Erle Stanley Gardner (Perry Mason, 1933), *The Roman Hat Mystery* by Ellery Queen (Ellery Queen, 1929), *The House Without a Key* by Earl Derr Biggers (Charlie Chan, 1925), *Whose Body?* by Dorothy L. Sayers (Lord Peter Wimsey, 1923), *The Mysterious Affair at Styles* by Agatha Christie (Hercule Poirot, 1920), and *The Maltese Falcon* by Dashiell Hammett (Sam Spade, 1930).

In most cases, the first edition can be identified only by confirming that title-page and copyright-page dates match. Most of these books go for average prices, but the more famous ones, such as *The Mysterious Affair at Styles,* will bring many times more, even without a dust jacket, which invariably enhances the value of a book to collectors. A first-edition copy of *The Maltese Falcon* brought $35 at a sale in 1972; only five years later an avid collector paid $750 for it.

The most valuable first editions are traditional hardbound volumes. But detective fiction, like many types of specialized popular literature, appears in other forms that have become collecting specialties, principally magazines and paperbacks. Many pulp magazines, so called because of the inexpensive paper they were printed on, are valuable. Among the most desirable of these is *Black Mask,* which introduced Dashiell Hammett's detective, Sam Spade, as well as many other famous fictional characters. Paperback first editions — published originally as paperbacks, and only later, if at all, in hard covers — of books written by Mickey Spillane, Ross Macdonald, Ellery Queen, Ed McBain and others offer the collector some relatively affordable prizes.

Paperbacks and old magazines are staples of the garage sale. For hardbound books, make it a point to attend college book sales, at which educational institutions raise money by selling books donated for the purpose by dedicated alumni. Dealers regularly line up early in the day to be first in the door when the selling starts. A friend of mine has reason to remember one sale of this sort. He was among the early risers one day for a college book sale and dashed to stake out turf inside as soon as the door opened. He was eagerly scanning a table when his eye rose to a bookshelf on the other side. There he caught a glimpse of something that seemed to be valuable. He could not tell what the book was, but somehow it "looked right." At the same instant, he realized that a dealer was making his way along that same shelf, checking the volumes spine by spine. My friend dived across the table and snatched the book; then he crashed to the floor, breaking a tooth.

The book? *Philo Gubb, Correspondence School Detective,* by Ellis Parker Butler, published in 1918. The college sale price was 25 cents and the value to a collector perhaps 100 times as much — a good but not superb find. The cost of repairing the broken tooth amounted to several hundred dollars.

For related material, see the article on Books in another volume of this encyclopedia.

156 / DETECTIVE FICTION

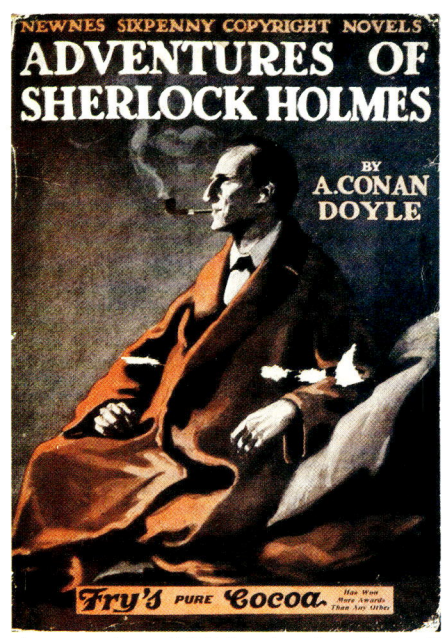

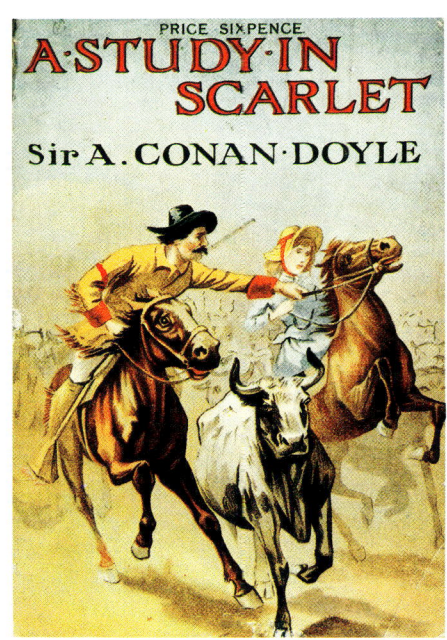

Among prizes of "Holmesiana"—the leading collectible of detective fiction—are these three items. At left is a paperback of the first Holmes stories, used to advertise cocoa. In the center is a 1906 edition of "A Study in Scarlet," its cover illustrating an American Wild West incident that provides the major clue. At right is a fake, a story having no connection with Holmes, published in Lisbon in 1905.

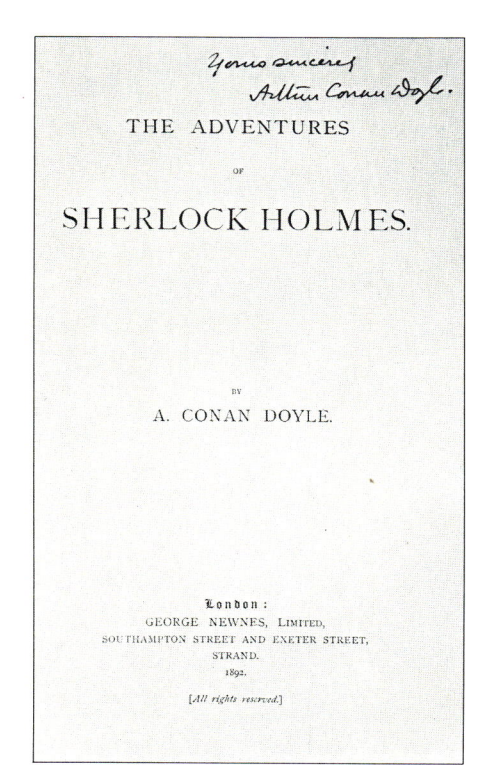

A copy of the first London edition of "The Adventures of Sherlock Holmes"—a U.S. edition appeared the same year, 1892—sold for more than $400 in 1978. The copy shown here is far more valuable than other first editions because it was signed by the author.

An original illustration by Sidney Paget for "The Musgrave Ritual" in "The Memoirs of Sherlock Holmes" is very desirable. Paget, the leading illustrator of Holmes stories, depicted the detective examining a clue and remarking sagely to Dr. Watson, "This really is something recherché."

Souvenirs of Sherlock

The most fanatic collectors of Holmesiana are so addicted to their mania that they collect even their own company, banding into groups to dine, strike medals, execute busts and in other ways proclaim their veneration of the consulting detective, sometime violinist and persistent cocaine user who shared the smoke-filled lodgings at 221B Baker Street with John H. Watson, M.D. There are more than 100 such groups in the United States, including The Baker Street Irregulars, the oldest and best-known of the associations devoted to Holmes; The Hounds of the Baskerville, in Chicago, and The Speckled Band of Boston. Another, The Adventuresses of Sherlock Holmes, was organized by women admirers of the great detective who were barred from the all-male Baker Street Irregulars.

The Irregulars—named after a band of urchins the detective employed to gather information in London's underworld—hold a dinner honoring Holmes's birthday, January 6, and have published *The Baker Street Journal*, a magazine on Holmesiana that itself is a collectible. In 1940 these mystery addicts became the subject of a mystery novel, *The Case of The Baker Street Irregulars* by Anthony Boucher, and it too is eminently collectible.

Holmes's deerstalker hat adorns a coin issued by The Scandalous Bohemians, Holmesiana collectors of New Jersey.

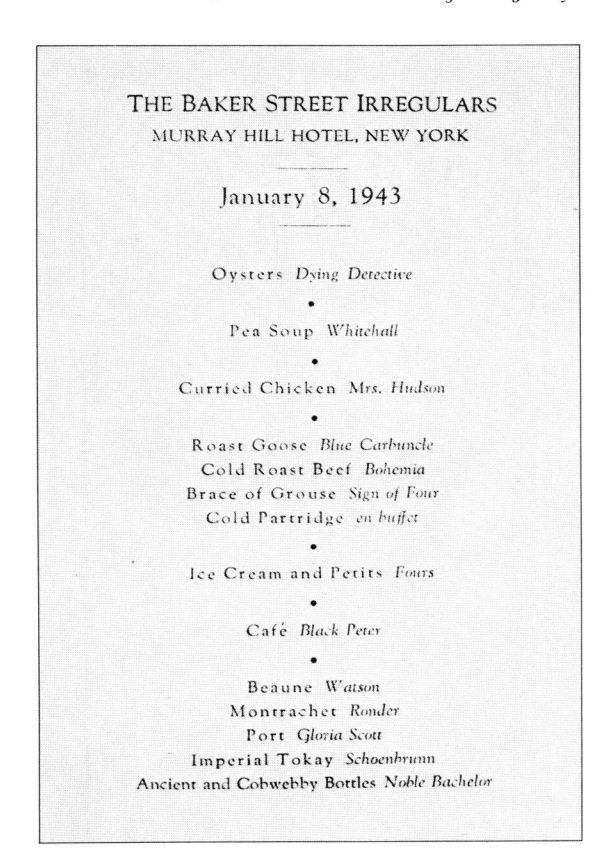

A 1943 dinner menu of Holmes fans, The Baker Street Irregulars, has dishes given names from Holmes stories.

This bust, one of 60 made for The Baker Street Irregulars, is said to copy one that helped trap the villain of "The Adventure of the Empty House."

158 / DETECTIVE FICTION

In 1934 Dashiell Hammett, founder of the hard-boiled-detective school of crime fiction, worked briefly on a comic strip called "Secret Agent X-9," which was drawn by Alex Raymond, creator of "Flash Gordon." This paperback is a rare compilation of the work.

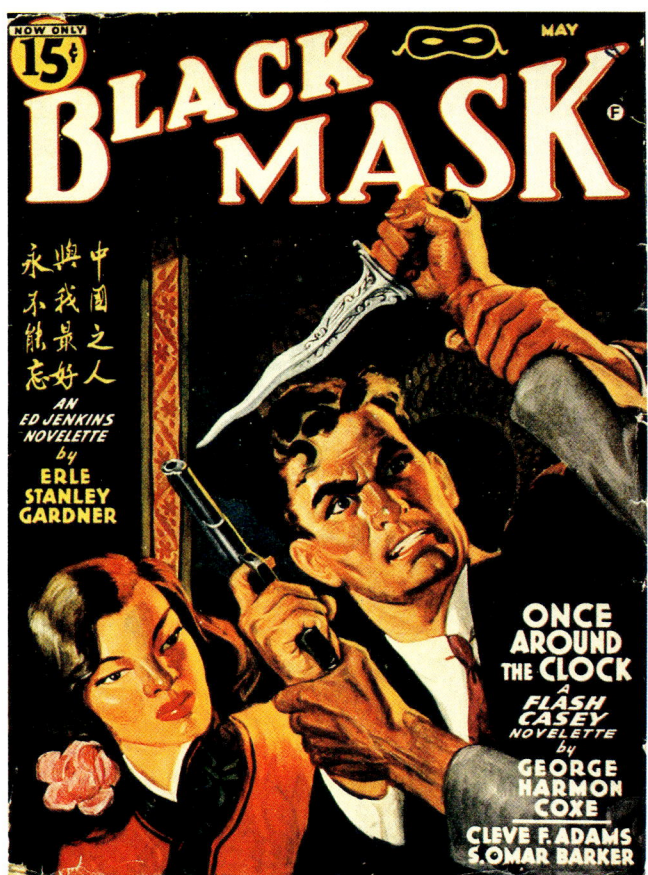

"Black Mask" magazine, a training ground for many celebrated American detective writers, including Dashiell Hammett and Raymond Chandler, is a collecting favorite. This 1941 issue of the pulp magazine contains, among other features, a Perry Mason story.

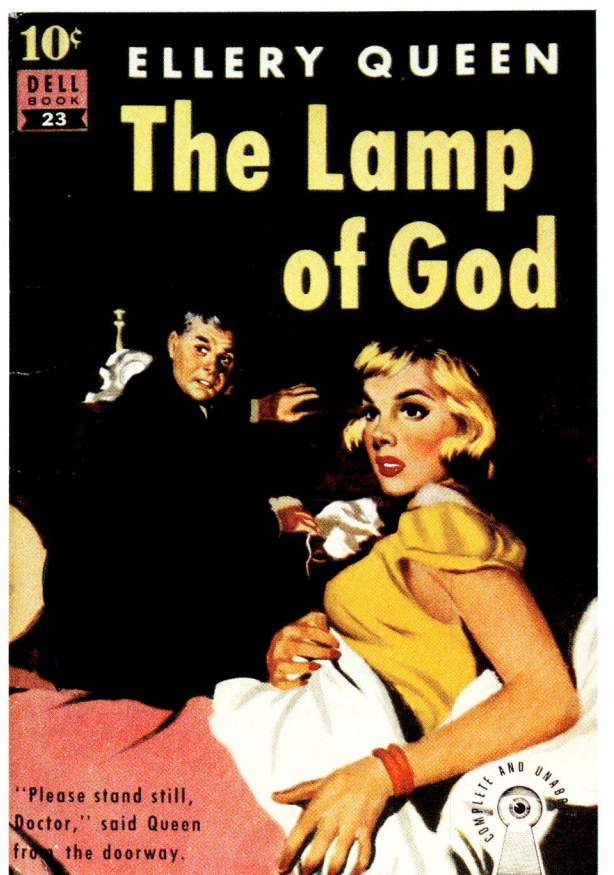

Low-priced paperbacks have become a collecting specialty. Above is an early short story by the collaborators who called themselves Ellery Queen. Dell published it for 10 cents in 1950, and over the years its value has increased more than 100 times.

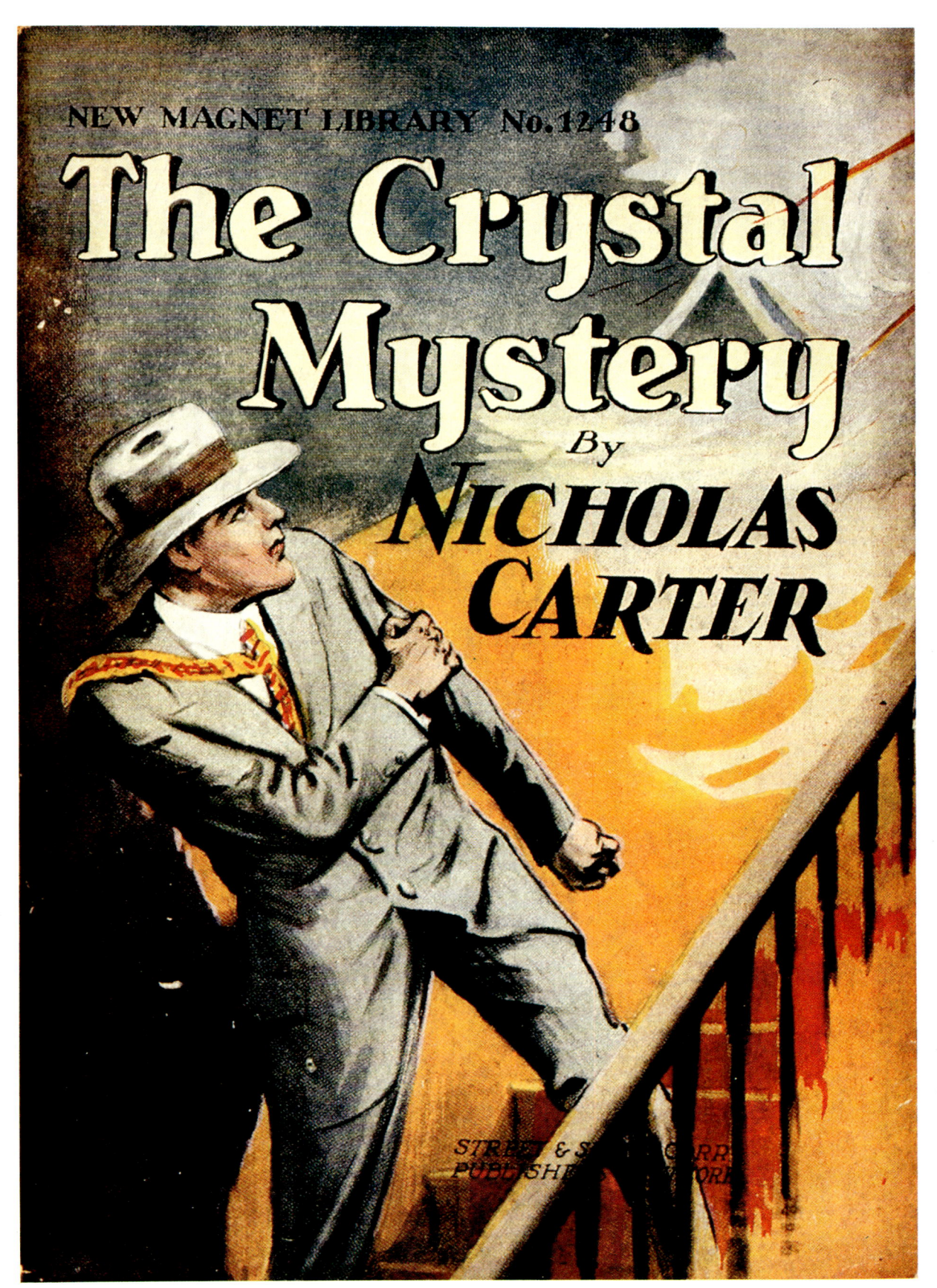

Nicholas Carter, who changed in character almost as frequently as the pseudonym shifted from writer to writer, began life as a teen-age detective in 1908 (above), then was reborn as an adult sleuth in 1939 and as a superspy in the 1960s.

160 / DETECTIVE FICTION

On the cover of a true murder story written in 18th Century China—the 1949 translation is by Robert van Gulik—Judge Dee (right) and Sergeant Hoong question under torture a lady accused of murdering her husband. She refused to confess, and Judge Dee proved her innocent.

Dr. Fu Manchu, Oriental archvillain par excellence, was invented by Sax Rohmer (a pseudonym for Arthur Sarsfield Ward) in 1913, when "The Insidious Dr. Fu Manchu" appeared. The title above appeared in 1959, the year that Rohmer died after a prolific writing career.

LIBRARIES
Humanities Research Center
The University of Texas
Austin, Texas 78712

Lilly Library
Indiana University
Bloomington, Indiana 47401

Occidental College Library
Occidental College
Los Angeles, California 90041

BOOKS
Barzun, Jacques, and Wendell Hertig Taylor, *A Catalogue of Crime*. Harper & Row, Publishers, 1971.

Haycraft, Howard, *Murder For Pleasure*. Biblo and Tannen, 1968.

Penzler, Otto, ed., *The Great Detectives*. Little, Brown & Company, 1978.

Penzler, Otto, *The Private Lives of Private Eyes, Spies, Crimefighters, and Other Good Guys*. Grosset & Dunlap, 1977.

Steinbrunner, Chris, and Otto Penzler, *Encyclopedia of Mystery and Detection*. McGraw-Hill Book Company, 1976.

Symons, Julian, *Mortal Consequences*. Schocken Books, 1973.

Winn, Dilys, *Murder Ink*. Workman Publishing Company, Inc., 1977.